CHANNELING
your
INNER BosS

CHANNELING
your
INNER
BosS

NICHOLAS MINSHALL

CHANNELING YOUR INNER BOSS

Copyright © 2019 by Nicholas Minshall

Part I

Personal Accountability

People who are able to define the personal values they hold most important discover what drives them to assume personal accountability for the results of their work.

Exploring Personal Accountability

Nearly every manager and employee is accountable to a supervisor, a director, or even a customer or client. Decisions about tasks, priorities, deadlines, and goals are made by someone else, an external authority who is often called "the boss."

Your external boss holds a position of power. The boss judges whether you've done a good job, whether you'll receive a raise in pay, and whether you'll hear praise or criticism.

However, there's another authority who holds even more power over an employee's work than an external boss. Employees are also accountable to their own values and conscience, their "inner boss."

Stan and Melanie are executives who work for a parcel delivery service. They have a lot in common:

- the same job title
- the same daily duties
- the same salary
- the same number of years on the job

Stan takes direction from his supervisor. He does exactly what his boss asks – no more, no less. He depends on his supervisor to tell him what to do and whether he's done the job correctly. Stan does the bare minimum his job requires of him.

Stan's Description 1

"I'm in charge of a department of more than 200 employees. It's my job to make sure everybody stays busy and meets individual deadlines."

Stan's Description 2

"I don't worry about how my department's work affects the rest of the company. We have senior managers who take care of that."

Like Stan, Melanie is accountable to her supervisor for her job performance. She's also accountable to herself. Melanie follows her own values and conscience in how she performs her work.

Melanie's Description 1

"It's my job to make sure our customer service agents have the information they need to locate any parcel in our delivery system. When our agents can locate parcels quickly, they can answer customers' questions and resolve any problems."

Melanie's Description 2

"I talk to my counterparts in the customer service department every week. They tell me about any problems they've had locating parcels in the system. That helps me find ways to improve the way my department works."

Reflect

Stan and Melanie are both accountable to external bosses. However, Melanie also applies her own values and personal standards to her job. She listens to an internal voice – an "inner boss" – that influences the way she performs her role. What are the important differences between the descriptions that Stan and Melanie give of their roles?

Peter Drucker, a theorist on organizations and management, wrote:

"The [employee] who focuses on efforts and who stresses his downward authority is a subordinate no matter how exalted his title and rank. But the [employee] who focuses on contribution and who takes responsibility for results, no matter how junior, is in the most literal sense of the phrase, 'top management.' He holds himself accountable for the performance of the whole."

Melanie focuses on the contribution she and her department make to the company's success. She holds herself accountable for the results of the whole company. Melanie exercises personal accountability.

People who are able to define the personal values they hold most important discover what drives them to assume personal accountability for the results of their work.

Defining the values that drive personal accountability provides several benefits.

First, making a contribution to an organization's goals based on deeply held personal values increases a person's estimation of the value of her work. She sees herself as contributing something important and valuable.

Second, acting on the basis of defined personal values gives a person more confidence in her own judgment. She's better able to exercise decision-making control over her own work.

Finally, people whose jobs fulfill personal values find their work more satisfying and rewarding.

Ruth is a buyer for a department store company. She has examined her personal values to learn what drives her to assume personal accountability for the results of her work. Ruth places high value on being able to express her creativity and entertain others.

Value

"Because I like to entertain people, I plan special events in our stores throughout the year. By making our stores entertaining places to shop, I contribute more to the success of our company than the average buyer."

Control

"When our stores show customers a constant stream of new merchandise presented in interesting ways, the customers come back to shop more often. In applying my creativity, I make better decisions about ways to increase customer traffic."

Satisfaction

"Some of the other buyers for this company see their jobs as managing merchandise. For me, my job is like show business. I see each sale event as a big show. The opportunity to use my creativity and love of entertaining makes this job perfect for me."

Personal accountability isn't something anyone can demand from you. It's something you create from within. In this lesson, you'll learn how to identify the personal values that provide your motivation for personal accountability.

2

Characteristics of Accountability

A distinguishing characteristic is any quality that sets one member of a group apart from all the rest.

People who practice personal accountability usually stand out in any organization. They display certain distinguishing characteristics that define how they relate to others in the organization around them:

- They define their relationship with the organization as a contribution toward the organization's goals.
- They acknowledge the impact that the quality of their work has on others.
- They answer for the success or failure of their own work.

Employees who practice personal accountability define their relationship with the rest of their organization in terms of a contribution toward the organization's goals. They display this characteristic in the way they describe the inputs to and the outputs from the work they perform.

Input

Input received from others is described as actions or needs that are part of a process. Input is not described as static documents or objects.

Output

The output from their own work is described as an input to the work of another member of the organization, or as a final product or service for a customer or client.

Cliff is a page designer for a popular news magazine. Maxine evaluates mortgage loan applications for a bank. Ben supervises the technical support agents who answer questions from a software company's customers. All these employees demonstrate personal accountability.

Different people demonstrate accountability in different ways. Here are different ways that people can describe their roles within their organizations.

Cliff

"After reporters write stories to explain the news and photographers show events in pictures, my contribution is to design pages that present the stories and pictures in a way that will grab the reader's attention and enhance the impact of the story."

Maxine

"A mortgage broker interviews a potential borrower and helps her prepare the application. That's where I come in. I analyze the borrower's credit history and income, and add my recommendation about the amount and terms of the loan our bank can offer."

Ben

"Our software testing team researches problems in our software. I receive the reports the testing team issues, and I make sure our technical support agents understand the reports and can help customers work around any problems with our products."

Another characteristic that distinguishes employees who practice personal accountability is their acknowledgement of the impact that the quality of their work has on others. They may describe how their work benefits someone else – a coworker or a customer – when the work is performed correctly. They may also describe how a coworker or customer is negatively affected when the work isn't done properly.

Cliff, Maxine, and Ben all acknowledge that the quality of their work affects other members of their organizations, or the organizations' customers.

The way that one demonstrates accountability directly affects the quality of their work within their organization.

Cliff

"A well-designed page helps the reader quickly understand what a story is about. If I design a page properly, our readers are more likely to notice and read a story our reporters and photographers have worked hard to cover."

Maxine

"If I don't evaluate a mortgage loan application correctly, the loan might be delayed or unfairly rejected. If it's delayed, our closing department will have to gather additional information. If it's rejected, we will lose a potential customer."

Ben

"If I keep my technical support agents well informed, they will be able to resolve the customers' problems with our products. If the customers think our products are reliable, they will continue to use them."

Employees who practice personal accountability are willing to answer for their own successes or failures. They accept praise when they succeed and criticism when they fail. They don't try to shift blame for poor results or make excuses.

In the workplace, you may answer to feedback from supervisors, coworkers, subordinates, or customers. Personal accountability means being willing to answer responsibly to anyone who offers feedback on your work results.

You need confidence and courage to answer for the success or failure of your own work. Many people are reluctant to seem boastful about their successes. They may be even more reluctant to shoulder the blame for a failure alone.

The way one demonstrates personal accountability, can often mean the difference between their work being a success or a failure.

Cliff

"Sometimes stories and photos are late. They often need more space or less space on the page than expected. Those problems don't change my job. I still have to make the page look great. It is my problem if the story isn't presented well."

Maxine

"The mortgage brokers who bring loan applications to me occasionally overlook evidence that a borrower isn't qualified for the loan he's seeking. In these cases, the responsibility for the decision is still mine. I have to make sure the bank loans its money wisely."

Ben

"My performance is judged by the customers' satisfaction with my department's service. Sometimes customers call with problems that our software testers have not investigated. It's still up to me to make sure the customers' problems are solved."

Employees who don't demonstrate the three characteristics of personal accountability are likely to show the opposite traits:

- They define their roles in the organization with activities or titles.
- They lack interest or knowledge about the impact that the quality of their work has on others.

- They claim credit they don't deserve and seek to blame others for failures.

Compare Cliff's earlier role description with a description that does not demonstrate personal accountability.

After reporters write stories to explain the news and photographers show events in pictures, my contribution is to design pages that present the stories and pictures in a way that will grab the reader's attention and enhance the impact of the story.

I'm a page designer. I decide where to place the stories and photos on the page, and what typestyles to use. I design the world news section of the magazine, so I'm in charge of one of the most important parts of the magazine.

Cliff's second description of his role focuses on activities and authority, not his contribution to the rest of the organization. He shows no interest in how his work affects others who must use it. Cliff is staying within his own narrowly defined boundaries.

If everyone in an organization worked this way, members of the organization would never interact with one another. The characteristics of personal accountability are the behaviors that connect the members of an organization.

Reflect

In what ways do you demonstrate the characteristics of personal accountability? In what ways do you sometimes fail to demonstrate these characteristics?

Employees who care about and enjoy their jobs stand out from the rest. They exhibit the characteristics of personal accountability. Do you?

3

Meeting Your Inner Boss

What kind of work would you be willing to do without pay? If you were working for free, why would you still be willing to work?

Your answer to these questions can help you discover the values that motivate you at work. If there's a job you would do without pay, then that type of work offers intangible rewards that are at least as valuable to you as money.

If your effort is inherently rewarding, you're hearing the voice of your inner boss. You're more likely to do a good job and accept accountability for the results when your responsibilities fulfill your motivating work values.

There are two steps for meeting your inner boss and learning what motivating work values drive you to become personally accountable for the results of your work:

- Describe your work preferences.
- Isolate your motivating work values.

The first step in meeting your inner boss is describing your work preferences. Your work preferences relate what your job would be like if you could have everything your way. Work preferences are the statements you would use to answer the question, What's important to you at work?

Imagining an ideal job, a job that would be a perfect fit for you, is one way to explore your work preferences. You may also describe what you like about your current job if you're happy in that job.

A complete description of your work preferences should include statements that address three aspects of your current or ideal job.

Contribution

A contribution statement describes what you believe is important to produce or accomplish through your work. Your contribution should benefit your organization, your coworkers, or your customers – not yourself.

Relationship

A relationship statement describes how you prefer to interact with your organization, coworkers, or customers. Relationship statements may describe whether you'd rather lead or follow, and whether you like to work alone or with a team.

Measurement

A measurement statement describes how you define success or failure in the work you perform. This statement should emphasize the observable responses of coworkers, supervisors, or customers instead of pay raises or changes in job title.

All three types of statements in a description of work preferences should be stated in positive terms. They should say what you want, or what you consider important, instead of what you'd like to avoid or prevent. The statements should describe ongoing conditions, not single events.

You may include more than one statement of each type in your description of work preferences. A complete description will include at least one statement of each type.

Byron, a reporter for a daily newspaper, is examining his work preferences. Here are some examples of work preference statements he could include.

"I enjoy working with an editor to plan the outline of a story and then working on my own to write the story."

This statement describes how Byron likes to work with editors, so it's a relationship statement.

"I know that I've done a good job writing a story when readers call or write with positive comments."

This statement describes observable behavior by readers that Byron can interpret as a sign of success, so it's a measurement statement.

"I like to dig into complicated situations and explain them so our readers can understand."

This statement describes the contribution Byron strives to make with his work; it's a contribution statement.

Here are two other statements that describe aspects of Byron's job that he considers important. Note that neither of these statements belongs in Byron's description of work preferences.

"One of my aspirations is to win a Best Story award from our state press association."

Winning an award is a measure of success, but it's a single event, not an ongoing condition that can happen day after day. Reader response is an ongoing condition.

"I avoid stories that require only a superficial reporting of events without an explanation of their causes."

By describing what Byron wanted to avoid, he used a negative statement to express a work preference for helping readers understand complex situations.

Reflect

Try writing a few work preference statements of your own. First, decide whether you want to describe what's important to you about your current job or an ideal job you think would be a perfect fit.

The second step in meeting your inner boss is isolating your motivating work values from your description of work preferences.

To isolate motivating work values, examine your work preference statements, and then ask yourself why each preference is important to you.

Your first answer to why a work preference is important may not be your final answer. Dig deeper by examining your first answer and asking the same question again: Why is this important to me? Repeat this process until you can explain your motivating work value in a terminal statement.

A terminal statement of a motivating work value explains how a work preference fulfills your own wants or needs. If your answer describes how your

Personal Accountability

preference benefits someone else, that's not a terminal statement.

Many kinds of work values motivate people to take work seriously and make a genuine effort to do a good job. Here are a few examples of motivating work values:

- accomplishment
- competition
- helping society
- making decisions
- creativity
- recognition
- problem solving
- teamwork

Now Byron knows how his inner boss influences his motivation and willingness to take accountability for his work. By following the two-step process, he uncovered many preferences and values, including:

- a work preference for measuring success by positive reader response
- a motivating work value of seeking confirmation of his intellectual status.

Reflect

Think about the work preferences you identified earlier. Ask yourself why those preferences are important to you. Keep asking yourself why until you arrive at terminal statements for several of your motivating work values. Try to record a few terminal statements of your motivating work values.

Stan has uncovered at least two of his motivating work values: striving for recognition as the best at his job and earning the respect of coworkers.

Other statements that are not terminal statements may yet lead Stan to discover more motivating values. He must dig more deeply and continue to question why those statements describe results that are important to him.

When you uncover your motivating work values, you discover your inner boss. You're listening to your own inner voice that gives you a reason to assume accountability for the work you do.

4

Your Inner Boss Meets the Real World

Working for two different bosses may create serious problems. When two separate authorities give you conflicting instructions, you can find yourself torn between them.

When you begin to pay attention to your personal motivating work values, you're choosing to work for two bosses: your inner boss and the supervisory authority in your real-world organization. You can avoid conflicts between your personal values and your organization's values by performing two steps:

- List the values practiced by your organization.
- Map the alignment of personal and organizational values.

The first step in understanding how your personal values interact with your organization's values is to list the values practiced by your organization.

Time

An investment of time is evidence of the values practiced by an organization. Each organization allocates time and effort to outcomes that it values.

Money

The way an organization allocates money is evidence of its values. If an organization spends money to achieve a result, the organization values that result.

Making a list of the values an organization practices isn't always easy. Some organizations don't practice what they promise. They may profess support for fine ideals and honorable corporate values, but the values they actually practice may be quite different.

When you're listing the values practiced by your organization, remember that words aren't evidence. The values leaders talk about or proclaim in documents such as mission statements aren't indicators of the values they really practice.

Karen works for a medical supply company. She's making a list of the values her company practices. She adds a value to the list only when she observes clear evidence that the company actually practices it.

Community Involvement

The company donates more than a million dollars each year to local charities. It allows employees to volunteer for community service projects on company time. Time and money donations are evidence that community involvement is a practiced value.

Humor and Fun

The company president often declares in meetings that work should be fun and incorporate humor. However, the company does not sponsor fun activities for employees. The mood in the office is very serious. The evidence does not support the president's declarations.

Accessibility

The company's code of conduct says senior executives are always accessible to any employee. In practice, middle managers block lower-level employees from approaching senior executives. The code of conduct is not evidence that accessibility is practiced.

Customer satisfaction

Customer satisfaction is a demonstrated organizational value. The company authorizes any employee to spend up to $5,000 to remedy a client's problem or complaint. No prior approval is required. This allocation of money is evidence of a practiced value.

Reflect

Think about the values your organization professes and the values it actually practices. What values does your organization practice? What evidence indicates that each value is practiced?

The next step in avoiding conflicts between your personal motivating work values and your organization's values is to map the alignment of these two sets of values. The more your personal values coincide with your organization's values, the less trouble you will have in acting according to your own values.

However, it's important to recognize differences between your own values and the values your company practices. If you recognize those differences, you'll be better prepared to develop strategies to avoid problems.

When you compare a list of your personal values with a list of the values practiced by your organization, each value will fall into one of four categories:

- alignment
- obligation
- opportunity
- conflict

You can map the alignment of personal values and organizational values to help you find how your motivating work values can help you take accountability for your work results. You may use a personal accountability map. This map is divided into four quadrants, one for each of the four categories.

Alignment

Values are in alignment when they appear on your list of personal values and are also practiced by your organization. Aligned values allow you to fulfill the organization's values while acting in accordance with your own inner boss.

Obligation

Obligations include values practiced by your organization, but not on your list of personal values. Organizations expect all members to observe shared values. To exercise personal accountability, you must find a way to act in accordance with obligation values.

Opportunity

Opportunity values are those included on your list of personal values, but not regularly practiced by your organization. These values provide an opening for you to act in accordance with your own conscience while exceeding the demands of your organization.

Conflict

Values are in conflict when a value on your list of personal values is incompatible with one of the organization's values. When a values conflict occurs, you must choose whether you will defer to the organization's values or assert your own values instead.

Wade is a lab technician for a company that develops genetically engineered food crops. He lists his organization's values and his personal values.

Organizational Values

The company values risk taking, experimentation, and adaptability to change. These values reflect attributes the organization needs in order to compete and survive.

Personal Values

Wade's personal values include using his knowledge and reasoning skills in creative and ethical ways. He hopes for a long career with the same company.

Innovation is a value the company practices to apply new scientific discoveries. Wade's creativity supports the company's need for innovation. These values are similar and dependent upon each other. They belong in the alignment quadrant.

Wade lists loyalty and risk taking as values the company practices. However, neither is on his list of motivating work values. If he is to practice personal accountability for his results, he has an obligation to honor these values.

Wade lists ethics and intellectualism among his personal values, but these are not on his list of organizational values. Wade can act on his own values to enhance his work and thereby become more accountable for his results.

Wade lists company stability as something he values. He recognizes that his company values adaptability to change, the opposite of stability. Honoring both values will be difficult or impossible.

Wade's careful examination of his own motivating work values helps him discover what he considers important in his work. Wade's evaluation of his company's values will help him identify what's important to his employer. When the personal values that motivate Wade align with the values practiced by his organization, he's more likely to receive acceptance and support for his actions. If there's a conflict, Wade must either conform to the organization's values or assert his own values and risk the consequences.

When a member of an organization is motivated to act by a value in alignment, the organization is very likely to accept and support that action. If Roger is motivated to act to enhance his affiliation, or sense of belonging, in the organization, that action aligns with the organization's values.

Members of organizations create additional alignments by pairing obligations with opportunities. If Roger can fulfill his need for security with an action that supports the organization's value for profit gain, he has created an alignment.

Reflect

Think about your personal motivating work values and the values practiced by your organization. What values are already in alignment? What pairings of opportunities and obligations can you use to create new alignments?

You can listen to the voice of your inner boss and practice your own values without creating conflicts. In fact, when you understand how your personal values align with your organization's values, conflicts are less likely.

5

Personal Accountability

When employees of business organizations are reluctant to assume personal accountability for their work, they're hiding. What do you think they're hiding from?

Putting personal accountability to work requires you to engage decision makers such as supervisors and colleagues in your organization about the way you want to do your job.

That takes courage. Many people avoid engaging decision makers. They fear that discussing their plans and activities will lead to poorly informed decisions and a loss of control over their own work.

When you don't involve decision makers with what you're doing, they're even more likely to make poorly informed decisions that make your job more difficult – the very thing you want to avoid. Engaging decision makers through personal accountability brings several benefits:

- You exercise more decision-making authority over your work.
- You gain validation for your plans and goals.
- You create opportunities to take credit for your successes.

Two benefits of personal accountability – exercising decision-making authority and gaining validation for your plans – give you more freedom in planning how you'll perform your job.

Decision-Making Control

When you make decisions about plans for your own work, others are likely to let those decisions stand. After all, you know your job better than anyone.

Validation

When you discuss your plans with supervisors or colleagues, they have a chance to voice their opinions. They're more likely to offer support and approval.

Some people think that practicing personal accountability is just a nice way of saying "accepting the blame."

But when you practice personal accountability, you take command of your own job. If you stand willing to accept responsibility for your own failures, it's also within your grasp to claim credit for your own successes.

Kate is a commodities purchaser for a manufacturer of breakfast cereal. A few months ago, she began making a conscious effort to practice personal accountability at work. Since then, Kate is much more satisfied with her job.

Decisions

"Instead of waiting for instructions from my supervisor, I make some decisions for myself. Most of the time, my supervisor agrees with my decisions and supports them."

Validation

"I seek out some of the other purchasers and tell them about decisions I'm considering. They often give me advice based on their experience. Their advice validates my plans and goals and lets me know my thinking is on the right track."

Credit

"When I include my supervisor and coworkers in my decision making, they know what goals I've set for myself. When I achieve those goals, they know it's because I've done the necessary work. I can take credit for my success."

Practicing personal accountability means there's no reason to hide from decision makers in your organization. When you take accountability for your plans, actions, and results, you need not fear losing control of your own job.

6

Putting Your Inner Boss in Charge

When a supervisor gives you an assignment, you expect the instructions to be clear. You shouldn't expect any less from your inner boss. When you apply your own values to the way you do your job, you need a clear plan.

Creating a plan for personal accountability prepares you to communicate with supervisors, coworkers, or subordinates about what they should expect from you. An accountability plan includes:

- a specific proposed contribution to the organization
- metrics for measuring success or failure
- limits to manage expectations.

The first element of an accountability plan is a specific proposed contribution to the organization.

A contribution may be something tangible such as a report, a piece of equipment, a product, or a financial gain. It may also be something intangible such as information, shared knowledge, or training for other organization members.

Whether your proposed contribution is tangible or intangible, it should be something specific that results from your work and that can be readily measured or counted. The employees of four different organizations proposed contributions for which they chose to be personally accountable.

Information Technology Manager

An information technology manager for a medical products company proposed creating a way to increase the accuracy of the company's inventory accounting. Her contribution can be measured in the reduction of inventory errors.

Insurance Claims Adjuster

A claims adjuster for an insurance company made a proposal to phone his accounting office at the end of every week to resolve problems with the claims he files. His contribution can be measured in the reduction of claims paid late.

Telecommunications Executive

A regional vice president for a telecommunications company proposed a committee to increase employee volunteerism. His contribution can be measured in the number of hours in employee time donated to community organizations.

Hospital Billing Specialist

A billing specialist in a hospital proposed to teach other clerical workers how to interpret codes used to designate the types of treatments the hospital offers. She can measure her contribution by counting the number of days it takes to train her coworkers.

Every proposed contribution to your organization should be chosen for good reasons. You want your accountability plan to remind you of why you chose the proposed accountability.

This plan should specify how your proposed contribution fulfills a personal value and a value practiced by your organization.

Each of the four employees who chose to be personally accountable for their contributions were motivated by personal values, and each of their contributions aligned with a value practiced by their organizations.

Information Technology Manager

The information technology manager will find satisfaction in developing an accurate way to track inventory because solving problems is a personal value. Her contribution aligns with her company's value for accuracy and precision work.

Insurance Claims Adjuster

The insurance claims adjuster is motivated to make follow-up calls to his accounting office because he values taking care of customers. His company also places a high value on customer-focused behavior.

Telecommunications Executive

The telecommunications executive wants to promote volunteerism because he is motivated by a personal value to help society. Encouraging volunteerism also builds the prestige of belonging to the organization, something the company values highly.

Hospital Billing Specialist

The hospital billing specialist will enjoy training her coworkers because she values being recognized as an expert at what she does. Her contribution is important to the hospital because the company values teamwork and cooperation among employees.

When you propose a contribution, describe the result you plan to achieve, not the effort that produces it. A proposed contribution should not be defined in terms of your job description or formal authority.

Acquiring responsibility for a result is not the same as producing that result. Deadlines or schedules can be included in your overall plan, but they're not part of an appropriate description of your proposed contribution.

Because Jim concentrated on the result he wants to achieve, how that result benefits his organization, and his own motive for pursuing it, he has created a clear picture of his proposed contribution.

Reflect

Try to describe a proposed contribution for which you will assume personal accountability. Remember to identify the personal value that motivates you and the value practiced by your organization that your contribution will support.

The second element of an accountability plan is a set of metrics. A success metric describes a standard for success that can be observed and then counted or measured. If this condition occurs, your contribution is successful.

Sometimes, failure means simply not achieving the success metric. In other cases, a different standard may define failure. Whether based on a success metric or other standard, specify your definition of failure.

An appropriate metric clearly describes the conditions of success from your contribution. Vague descriptions of improvement, increased knowledge, or improved service don't specify conditions that can be observed. If you can't see it, you can't measure it.

Statements that confuse effort with result are also inappropriate success metrics. The amount of work that goes into a contribution isn't a measure of whether you achieve the desired result.

Each of the four employees who proposed contributions to their organizations set appropriate metrics to determine whether they succeeded or failed.

Information Technology Manager

The information technology manager defines success as reducing the difference between inventory records and actual equipment on hand to less than 1 percent. She defines failure as not implementing the new system before the end of the fiscal year.

Insurance Claims Adjuster

The insurance claims adjuster defines success as reducing the number of delayed payments to policy holders to less than 5 percent of all payments. If he doesn't reduce late payments to less than 5 percent, he has failed.

Telecommunications Executive

The telecommunications executive thinks he can persuade company employees to donate a total of 2,000 hours to community organizations in one year. That's his success metric. However, he'll consider his project a failure if employees donate less than 500 hours.

Hospital Billing Specialist

The hospital billing specialist set a success metric to train all of her coworkers within 60 days. She defines failure as leaving some of her coworkers untrained at the end of 90 days.

Jim applied just one standard for both success and failure. If he completes his contribution within 45 days, he will have succeeded. If he doesn't, he will have failed to achieve his proposed contribution.

Reflect

How do you define success and failure for your proposed contribution within your organization?

Some workers are reluctant to propose a specific contribution or to take on new responsibilities. They're afraid that taking on more responsibilities will encourage supervisors or coworkers to keep raising their expectations. They fear that a small contribution may become an overwhelming burden.

That's why the third element of an accountability plan entails defining limits to manage expectations. When you propose a contribution, you don't have to open the door to unlimited new demands from the rest of your organization.

One way to set limits to manage expectations is to clearly describe the last step in the contribution you'll make. When you complete that step, you can hand off responsibility for the results of your work.

Another way to set limits is to identify specific exclusions from your proposed contribution. If your contribution affects only some coworkers or customers, or is otherwise limited, be sure to spell out what's not included.

Describe limits on a proposed contribution in terms of your own actions, not actions that might be expected of others. Limits should draw the line between the actions you'll perform and those you won't perform.

You can leave decisions about actions expected from others to your supervisor or other managers. The actions of others aren't part of your personal accountability.

The four employees who proposed contributions to their organizations defined limits to manage the expectations of other members of their companies. They didn't want supervisors or coworkers to expect more than they were willing to contribute.

Information Technology Manager

The information technology manager described the last step she would perform in a new inventory system. She would balance the weekly inventory report against independent data from the company's purchasing system.

Insurance Claims Adjuster

The insurance claims adjuster described the last step in his proposed contribution as correcting any claims authorizations with missing data. He excluded claims over $100,000 from his proposal because they follow a different payment process.

Telecommunications Executive

The telecommunications executive described his last step in encouraging employee volunteerism: He will hold a kick-off meeting to begin each volunteer project. He also specifically excluded projects sponsored by political organizations.

Billing Specialist

The billing specialist limited her proposed contribution by identifying specific exclusions. She excluded part-time and temporary employees of the billing department from her planned training on hospital treatment codes.

If Jim does not set limits on his proposed contribution, other members of his organization may expect more from him than he intended to offer. By specifically excluding e-mail addresses for groups or departments, he avoids criticism from people who may have expected those addresses to change.

Specifying notification to e-mail users as his last step limits the scope of the work others should expect from him.

Reflect

Now set some limits on a proposed contribution of your own. How might others in your organization misinterpret the scope of your proposed contribution? Define a last step or specify exclusions to clarify your contribution.

Practicing personal accountability requires careful thought and planning.

The three elements of an accountability plan allow you to choose what you will contribute, how you will measure your success, and how you will set limits on your contribution to avoid misunderstandings.

7

Your Inner Boss in Action

Working for your inner boss turns the traditional hierarchy of an organization upside down.

When you assume personal accountability for your own work, you're turning the usual top-down flow of supervision on its head. You're taking responsibility for setting your own direction and your own goals instead of waiting for instructions from above.

This reversal can make other members of your organization uncomfortable. To make the reversal work, you'll have to explain your accountability plan and gain validation from supervisors or coworkers who are affected by it.

There are three steps you should perform in order to pitch your accountability plan to others and win validation of your plan:

- Test the language of your proposal.
- Describe your planned contribution briefly.
- Ask for approval of your accountability plan.

The validation of your supervisor or co-workers is the authorization you need to allow your inner boss to guide your work. Without validation, your plan can be easily derailed by others in your organization.

Pitching your plan is more likely to be successful when you complete a step before you begin a next one.

Test the language

The language you use to describe your plan can raise warning flags. Specific terms like contribution or accountability may have different connotations in different organizations. Test your language to find terms that elicit a positive response.

Describe your contribution

The second step is describing your contribution. This description should be brief, but it should include the problem you will address, the actions you will take, and the benefit to your organization. Your description may prompt questions or suggestions.

Ask for approval

The final step is asking for approval to implement your plan. Asking for approval gives you an opportunity to resolve any differences between your own goals and the organization's objectives. When you receive approval, you've won the authority to act.

Lisa is a junior producer for the evening news program at a television station. The station had a problem with errors in the on-screen captions that identify people appearing in news stories. Lisa planned to assume accountability for the accuracy of the captions.

She pitched her accountability plan to the news director. First, Lisa tested the language of her proposal by telling him she could contribute to a smoother-running broadcast.

If Lisa had thought the news director showed a negative response to the way she introduced her plan, she would have changed her terminology and tried again. When the news director showed a positive response, Lisa took that as a sign to continue with the next steps.

Describe your contribution

Lisa described the problems with the accuracy of the captions, the actions she planned to take, and the benefits those actions would bring to the news program.

Ask for approval

She answered the news director's questions and addressed any objections he raised. Only then did Lisa ask for his approval to implement her plan.

You may need to make a pitch for validation of your accountability plan to supervisors, peer-level coworkers, subordinates, or some other group of members in your organization. Your pitch should be made to whoever is affected by your work output, whoever will evaluate your work, and anyone whose approval is needed before you can act.

When you begin a pitch to gain validation of your accountability plan, test the language you will use to describe what you want to talk about. Some listeners may feel comfortable talking about an "offer," while others feel more at ease discussing a "contribution" or an "accountability."

List 1

Use words that convey your plan to take action and provide a benefit. Frame your discussion in terms of what you want to provide to the organization.

List 2

Avoid words that sound as though you're interested in your status or power instead of your actions. Don't describe what you want instead of what you have to offer.

When you test your language, you'll know you've found an appropriate term when your listener responds positively. A positive response may include the listener repeating the term back to you or simply expressing a willingness to discuss it.

When a listener responds negatively, try again using a different term. Negative responses can include trying to end or delay the conversation, declaring the topic off limits, or restating the term using negative words.

L eah is a children's book buyer for a chain of
bookstores. Follow along as she tests her
language to pitch an accountability plan to Joyce, her
supervisor.

Leah: Joyce, the company has been looking for
new ideas for special events in our stores. I have a
contribution I'd like to make.

Joyce: Leah, you're a buyer. Special events aren't
part of your responsibility. Let the marketing
department handle that.

   Leah should rethink the way she's approaching her
discussion with Joyce and test a different term. She
shouldn't try to go ahead and describe her proposed
contribution until she finds a term – not
"contribution" –that elicits a positive reaction from
Joyce and doesn't provoke her resistance.

L eah tried using different language to reopen her
conversation with Joyce. Follow along as they
continue their conversation.

Leah: I understand, Joyce. I'd like to offer my
participation in what the marketing department is
trying to accomplish for the company.
Joyce: I'm sure the marketing department would
welcome your participation in its events. What did
you have in mind?

Joyce responded positively this time. She mirrored Leah's use of the word "participation" and asked Leah for more information. Now Leah can continue to describe her proposed contribution.

When you describe your proposed contribution, put it in the form of a very, very brief story. Start with a description of a problem or situation that needs attention. Describe the actions you propose to take. Finish by stating how your actions will benefit the organization.

Don't overwhelm your listener with too many details at this point. Give the listener just enough information to understand what you're proposing. Let the details emerge as you respond to your listener's questions and reactions.

L eah wants to describe her proposed participation in special events. Follow along as she describes it to Joyce.

Leah: The marketing department wants to build traffic in the children's section during lunch hours. That's one of our slowest times.

Joyce: That's right. The stores are full of businesspeople on lunch break.

Leah: I would like to implement a weekly story hour in the children's section during lunch hour. I can use that time to introduce new children's books to any parents who are in the store.

Joyce: I don't know. That sounds like a lot of work for you.

Leah: The stores would get more of their lunch hour customers to visit the children's section and increase their sales.

After Leah has described her story time proposal, Joyce may ask questions or raise objections. Leah can fill in the details and respond to any of Joyce's concerns.

If Leah feels she has been successful in presenting her proposal, she can ask for Joyce's approval to proceed.

There are two types of questions you can use to ask for approval for an accountability plan: open-ended and closed-ended.

Open-ended

An open-ended question can't be answered with a simple yes or no. Open-ended questions often begin with words like "what," "how," or "why."

Closed-ended

Closed-ended questions have just a few possible answers: yes or no, up or down, left or right. They begin with phrases like "will you," "may I," or "which one."

You can use an open-ended question as a trial ending for your conversation. By asking an open-ended question when the conversation seems to be winding down, you invite your listener to bring up any remaining questions or objections.

Follow your open-ended question with a direct, closed-ended question that asks for approval of your plan. Phrase the question in a way that requests a positive answer, such as "Do you approve?" or "May I have your permission?"

Leah followed the steps in order to present her accountability plan and win her supervisor's approval to act on it. Leah chose her own goal and methods for achieving that goal. Now she has the authorization to pursue her plan.

If you followed the steps correctly, you tested your language by describing an accountability plan as an offer. When Darryl mirrored your language and said he was willing to hear the offer, you were able to describe the plan, discuss it, and ask for Darryl's approval to forge ahead.

If you didn't follow the steps in order or didn't perform them properly, there were many opportunities for Darryl's approval to slip away.

When you devise a plan to put your inner boss in charge of your work, you have to present your plan to the decision makers within your organization. Gaining validation of your plan from those decision makers allows you to close the deal between your inner boss and your organization.

8

Performance Review with Your Inner Boss

Erica is an executive in the traffic and scheduling department of a major airline. She often claims that she's her own worst critic.

Actually, that's a sign of her practice of personal accountability. Being answerable for the results of your own work requires you to take a hard, honest look at what you have accomplished.

Like any other boss, your inner boss demands an occasional performance review. This is when you tally your successes and failures and decide what to do next. Self-assessment isn't always a private matter. Often, you must communicate your self-assessment to others in your organization. That's how you answer for the results of your work.

Your presentation of a self-assessment should communicate a confident message, one that lets others know you're accountable for your work and will continue to be accountable for it.

Reflect

Many people fear assessment of their work because they feel they don't get credit for their successes and receive blame for failures. What strategies do you use to overcome the fear of honestly assessing your own work in front of others?

The whole point of assuming personal accountability is to take control and responsibility for your own work. The same notions apply to performing an accountability self-assessment. You can take control over your self-assessment before any audience by performing three steps:

- Claim credit for your successes.
- Accept responsibility for your shortcomings.
- Outline your plans for the future.

Each of the steps in an accountability self-assessment is characterized by a certain type of statement.

Claiming Credit

A statement to claim credit for success describes goals that were achieved or where you made significant progress. Examples include "I completed my report on time" or "I performed 11 of the 15 tests successfully."

Accepting Shortcomings

A statement to accept shortcomings admits to goals that were not achieved or where no significant progress was made. Examples include "I did not send my report to all of the executives on the distribution list" or "I failed to perform 4 of the 15 tests."

Outlining the Future

A statement to outline the future describes what you will do next to expand on your accountability. Examples include "I will incorporate the executives' comments into my final report" or "I will schedule the remaining tests."

Claiming credit for your successes is the rewarding part of an accountability self-assessment. First, restate what you set out to accomplish in just a few words. This avoids letting your listener expect too much or too little. Then, describe what you've accomplished.

You may fear that you'll look like you're boasting if you claim credit for your successes. Be bold. When you claim your successes, you inner boss is giving you a good review.

Follow along as Al, a purchasing manager for a tire maker, gives a self-assessment on a plan to reduce the time his department takes to pay invoices.

"I took accountability to reduce the time it takes us to process invoices."

"I succeeded in reducing the processing time for our European division and our U.S. division."

The first part of Al's statements restated his goal —
to reduce invoice processing time. The second part of
his statements described his success in two of the
company's divisions.

Accepting responsibility for shortcomings in your
work opens the door for criticism. But by taking the
lead in describing your shortcomings, you can actually
fend off criticism. It shows you're aware of problems
and failures.

Describe goals that you failed to achieve or where
no significant progress was made. Report the causes,
but don't blame others. Talk about the lessons you
learned from your problems or failures.

Al, the purchasing manager for the tire maker,
continues his accountability self-assessment. The
following statements relate to how Al accepted
responsibility for the shortcomings in his personal
performance.

Describe unachieved goals

"I failed to reduce the invoice processing
time for our Asian division because that
division uses a different format for electronic
invoices from the one in Europe"

Report causes

"I learned that we're not applying the same
standards in all divisions, and this creates
delays in invoice processing."

Al's first statement described the goal he failed to achieve in the company's Asian division. He explained the reason without casting any blame. His next statement revealed the lessons he learned about electronic invoice formats.

Close your accountability self-assessment by outlining the future. Accountability for your work doesn't end when you hand off a work product to a colleague or complete an assignment. Outlining the future gives you an opportunity to explain how you'll address shortcomings.

This demonstrates to your listener that your accountability continues, and it gives you a chance to exercise even more control over your own work.

Describe any proposed changes in goals, timelines, or activities. Tell your listener how these changes will affect the organization. Finally, ask for the help or collaboration you need to correct shortcomings and achieve your goals.

Al, the purchasing manager for the tire maker, outlines the future of his accountability to close his self-assessment. Follow along.

I plan to investigate two alternatives. The first is changing the invoice format used by the Asian division. The second is evaluating the cost of programming changes in our accounting system to convert invoice formats.

Either choice will require changes in the way we process all of our invoices, which will involve an amendment to our budget.

I'll need collaboration from the budget committee to evaluate these alternatives.

Al's statement to outline the future described the changes to the invoice processing system that he's considering. He noted the effect of these changes and asked for help from the budgeting committee.

If Pete followed the three steps for presenting an accountability self-assessment correctly, he could tell his story clearly, exercise some control over the conversation, and best of all, keep his inner boss in charge of his work.

If you didn't follow the steps for presenting an accountability self-assessment properly, Eleanor might have come to the conclusion that you had failed in trying to exercise personal accountability.

However, following the steps and performing them well allows you to tell your story and give yourself the most favorable review possible.

Sometimes it pays to be your own worst critic. If you take the job, you won't have to leave it to anyone else.

Personal Accountability

Part II

Managing from Within

Some experts report that our minds process thoughts at a rate of 500 to 600 words per minute. Not all of these words are positive or encouraging. Some of this internal dialogue is negative and self-defeating.

9

Empowering Yourself

Have you ever thought that you could be the best boss you've ever had? By developing attitudes and skills that empower you, you can manage from within and become your own best boss. You already know the person who will lead the way to self-empowerment: it's you!

Self-empowerment is the process of taking responsibility for your attitudes, behaviors, and actions at work to maximize your effectiveness.

As an empowered employee, you will be driven by ownership, initiative, and performance.

Hannah is a web designer who is interested in vying for a newly created team lead position. She may talk herself out of applying for the position because she believes that she doesn't have a chance. She thinks her supervisor and colleagues don't see her as a leader. Hannah is at risk of defeating herself with her own internal dialogue.

Hannah's perception couldn't be farther from the truth. Her supervisor and coworkers view her as a competent professional with excellent planning skills and the ability to motivate others to meet their objectives and deadlines.

Reflect

Many people can relate to Hannah's experience. Her self-defeating internal dialogue is holding her back at work. Think about a time when your internal dialogue impeded your professional success.

Like Hannah, you might not be aware of the subtle effect of self-defeating thoughts that prevent you from achieving at work. You may be an unsuspecting victim of your own internal dialogue. How you talk to yourself has a direct relationship to your sense of power in the world.

Recognize Self-Defeating Thoughts

When you lack self-empowerment, it is likely that you have an outspoken internal critic. Self-defeating internal dialogue leads to a sense of powerlessness. A self-empowered attitude helps you recognize and question your negative thinking patterns.

Develop A Self-Empowering Mind-Set

A self-empowering mind-set allows you to screen self-defeating thoughts. Gaining a self-empowering mind-set involves replacing negative internal dialogue with positive, reinforcing, and encouraging dialogue.

Become Your Own Best Coach

By mastering self-empowerment techniques, you can become your own best coach. You can use positive and encouraging messages to improve your ability to focus, learn, and perform.

Focus On Your Strengths And Goals

Self-empowerment helps you shift your focus away from your shortcomings and weaknesses. Instead, you can concentrate on your strengths and goals. Your energy is spent on attaining your goals rather than trying to overcome your self-doubts.

If Hannah lets her internal dialogue dictate her actions, she won't even apply for the team lead position. But what if Hannah were to use self-empowerment strategies to overcome her self-defeating internal dialogue?

Recognizing Thoughts

Hannah recognizes her self-defeating thoughts by taking time to listen. She notices that her internal dialogue is based on unfounded assumptions about how her supervisor and colleagues view her leadership potential.

Developing The Right Mind-Set

Once Hannah has identified the primary self-defeating thought – that she will never get the team lead position – she learns to combat her negative internal dialogue by developing a self-empowering mind-set. She replaces negative dialogue with positive dialogue.

Becoming A Coach

Instead of repeating messages that hold her back, Hannah consciously formulates coaching messages. In this case, she tells herself that she has the skills, ability, and drive to be a contender for the team lead position.

Focusing On Goals

Hannah focuses on her goal – to become a team lead – and her strengths: creativity, dependability, planning, motivation, and organization. By focusing on her strengths and goals, Hannah begins to believe that she is a strong candidate for the position.

Hannah's internal dialogue caused her to doubt herself, and it nearly prevented her from pursuing a professional advancement opportunity.

Self-empowerment helped Hannah recognize her self-defeating thoughts, replace negative internal dialogue with positive dialogue, become her own coach, and focus attention on her strengths and goals.

Like Hannah, you can succeed by empowering yourself.

In this lesson, you will learn to monitor your inner dialogue and become your own best coach. These approaches will lay the foundation for self-empowered attitudes and behaviors.

10

Monitoring Your Inner Dialogue

Some experts report that our minds process thoughts at a rate of 500 to 600 words per minute. Not all of these words are positive or encouraging. Some of this internal dialogue is negative and self-defeating.

Start listening to your own internal dialogue. You may be surprised by what you discover.

Once you're aware of your self-defeating dialogue, you can then choose to substitute it with positive, confident, and empowering thoughts.

Monitoring your self-defeating internal dialogue starts with being able to label the types of dialogue. Self-defeating dialogue usually triggers a negative mood state, such as anxiety or depression. You will most likely experience the mood state before you notice the self-defeating internal dialogue.

Emotional Reasoning

Emotional reasoning is believing that your negative feelings are an accurate reflection of reality.

Personalization

When your thinking is distorted by personalization, you see yourself as the cause of some negative external event that, in fact, you were not primarily responsible for.

Mind Reading

Mind reading is concluding, without evidence, that someone is responding negatively to you.

Catastrophizing

When you catastrophize, you anticipate the worst possible scenario for a given situation.

Perfectionism

Perfectionism is believing that unless you perform perfectly, you are a failure.

Emotional reasoning is likely to occur when a person suffers from low self-esteem or is feeling discouraged. People with healthy self-esteem know that their self-defeating feelings aren't usually an accurate reflection of reality. When experiencing emotional reasoning, you believe that because you feel something, it must be true. For example, if you feel inferior to others at work, you conclude that you are a second-rate person.

When you personalize, you jump to conclusions without reasonable evidence. For example, you may

Managing from Within

overhear a conversation at work and assume that it is about you.

To monitor your inner dialogue successfully, you must be able to distinguish between self-defeating and rational thoughts. It is common to have moments of self-doubt, but it's counterproductive to let self-doubt spiral out of control in the form of self-defeating internal dialogue.

Emotional reasoning: negative

With emotional reasoning, you might think, "When I'm asked to lead meetings, I feel incompetent, which must mean that I am incompetent. I'm going to avoid leading meetings at all costs."

Emotional reasoning: positive

You can turn emotional reasoning into positive thinking: "When I'm asked to lead meetings, I feel incompetent. But I know that my feelings aren't an accurate reflection of reality. I'll volunteer to lead meetings so I become more comfortable with the task."

Personalization: negative

With personalization, you may think, "As a new supervisor, I've made some mistakes. If I did a better job of supervising my employees, my assistant wouldn't be having problems affecting his performance. I should be able to prevent my employees' problems."

Personalization: positive

You can turn personalization into positive thinking: "As a new supervisor, I've made some mistakes. But I've done the best I could. I'm not the reason my assistant is having problems affecting his performance. The problems he's having are beyond my control."

If you engage in self-defeating internal dialogue, it may make you begin to doubt yourself. But when you change that internal dialogue, your thinking will become productive and useful.

Now, consider mind reading.

When you engage in mind reading, you make assumptions about other people's feelings and motivations, particularly as they relate to you. These assumptions stem from intuitions or hunches, but they should not be treated as fact.

Bridget is a project manager. She has started to feel that Jake, another project manager, questions her competence.

Mind reading

"Jake often interrupts me during meetings. He thinks I have nothing valuable to contribute."

Rational thinking

"Jake often interrupts me during meetings. I should observe his behavior with others. Perhaps interrupting is part of his communication style."

When you catastrophize, you predict a worst-case outcome in the future, without considering more likely outcomes. Catastrophic thinking is easy to recognize in that you predict a catastrophe that is unlikely to happen.

Bridget, the project manager, is preparing for a project management certification exam. She is worried about how she will perform on the exam.

Catastrophizing

"If I perform poorly on my certification exam, I'll never work again."

Rational thinking

"If I perform poorly on my certification exam, I'll study harder the next time and take it again."

As a perfectionist, you set unattainable standards and then fail to meet those standards. The result is a feeling that you are not good enough to meet your own or others' expectations.

Perfectionists think that minor mistakes or errors are intolerable and a reflection of failure.

Bridget, the project manager, is driven and detail oriented. She is working on a very tight deadline right now.

Perfectionism

> "If I miss my deadline on this project, I'll feel like a disappointment to my team and a total failure at work."

Rational thinking

> "If I miss my deadline, I'll finish my work as quickly as possible. I can't do everything perfectly. It's acceptable to me to do the best I can."

Now that you can differentiate among the various types of self-defeating internal dialogue, think about replacing that kind of thinking with rational thoughts.

11

Becoming Your Own Best Coach

By removing inner obstacles such as self-defeating internal dialogue, you can dramatically improve your ability to focus, learn, and perform – all actions that will help you become self-empowered.

Self-empowerment begins with becoming aware of the dialogue you have with yourself. Self-coaching is motivating yourself to succeed through the repetition of affirming and encouraging thoughts.

Step 1: Become aware

The first step is to become aware of your self-defeating internal dialogue. If you are feeling anxious or depressed when you think about a work-related issue or activity, it is a sign that your internal dialogue is getting you down.

Step 2: Label dialogue

The second step is to label the self-defeating internal dialogue. Label your dialogue as one of the five types of self-defeating internal dialogue.

Step 3: Apply self-coaching

The third step is to replace the self-defeating internal dialogue with the language of self-coaching. Identify positive, beneficial statements you can use to replace your negative, harmful thoughts.

Because self-defeating internal dialogue is automatic in many cases, it takes practice to effectively stop it. The more you practice, the better you'll be at interrupting self-defeating thoughts before they lead to inaction. Learn how to apply the three steps for replacing self-defeating internal dialogue with the language of self-coaching.

Become Aware

The first step is to notice your dialogue. Without awareness, you believe the dialogue is real and act accordingly. In some cases, it might paralyze you; in others, you may proceed in spite of it. The best course of action is to stop the self-defeating internal dialogue.

Label

After you have recognized that you are engaged in self-defeating internal dialogue, identify and label the type of dialogue. This will help you perform the third step. Knowing the characteristics of the five types of self-defeating internal dialogue will enable you to label each correctly.

Replace

To perform the third step, replace the self-defeating internal dialogue with the language of self-coaching. This language should be encouraging and focused on what you need to do to perform well. It should not be overly optimistic as to be implausible, and it should not require others' approval.

F ollow along as Will, a project team member, responds to a colleague without an awareness of his self-defeating internal dialogue.

Jodie: Did you hear that the project manager on the Wilson account is shortening the timeline and doubling the order?

Will: You're kidding, right?

Jodie: Nope. That's the latest from the conference call with the client.

Will thinking: This stinks. They always want higher quality work more quickly.

Will thinking: They're probably doing this to set us up for failure so that when it comes time to lay people off, they'll have rationale.

Will thinking: Not only am I not going to work harder and faster only to be laid off, but I'm going to spend time looking for a new job.

Will: Hmm. They'll have to choose between quality and speed. It's not possible to have both.

Did you notice how Will's self-defeating internal dialogue quickly led to thoughts of the worst-case scenario and negatively affected his morale and motivation?

Without an awareness of and an attempt to stop his self-defeating internal dialogue, Will's pessimism took hold and caused him to resist the client's request.

N ow, observe the same interaction as Will applies the steps for replacing self-defeating internal dialogue with the language of self-coaching.

Jodie: Did you hear that the project manager on the Wilson account is shortening the timeline and doubling the order?

Will: You're kidding, right?

Jodie: Nope. That's the latest from the conference call with the client.

Will thinking: This stinks. They always want higher quality work more quickly. They're probably doing this to set us up for failure so that when it comes time to lay people off, they'll have rationale.

Will thinking: Wait a second. I'm catastrophizing. It's probably not about layoffs. The client probably pushed back on management, so it's not the managers' fault. I'm just as interested in making the client happy as they are.

Will thinking: I can find a way to make this work. I've tackled short timelines before. And, although it required longer hours, in the end, we were rewarded.

Will: No problem. It'll be crazy around here. We'll make more coffee runs than usual, but we'll make it work!

Will became aware of his self-defeating internal dialogue, stopped it, and replaced it with the language of self-coaching. He coached himself to act with a positive, can-do attitude.

It's important to replace self-defeating internal dialogue with the language of self-coaching. If the dialogue is not stopped, your morale, attitudes, and actions can be negatively affected. In some cases, it may immobilize you.

Imagine if your internal dialogue, which consists of 500 to 600 words per minute, was positive and encouraging. You would become the best coach you've ever had.

By following the steps for replacing self-defeating internal dialogue with the language of self-coaching, you can achieve this goal.

12

Developing an Empowered Attitude

Did you know that you could have the job of your dreams right now?

There are many benefits of developing an empowered attitude.

Developing an empowered attitude:

- increases your sense of job ownership
- helps you transition from employee to entrepreneur
- assists you in turning complaints into solutions

- increases your involvement at work.

A person with an empowered attitude has a positive, action-oriented mind-set and seeks solutions to problems.

Increases your sense of job ownership

An empowered attitude increases your commitment to your job. Your job becomes no longer just a job that belongs to your company, but rather one that belongs to both you and your company. You see yourself as a partner aligned with your company's mission and goals.

Helps you transition from employee to entrepreneur

An empowered attitude helps you see yourself as an entrepreneur, where you look for ways to acquire the resources you need to achieve your goals.

Assists you in turning complaints into solutions

An empowered attitude helps you respond to problems and issues in a solutions-oriented way. Rather than complaining about problems, you generate solutions that can benefit both you and your company.

Increases your involvement at work

An empowered attitude increases your involvement at work. With such an attitude, you actively participate in your company's efforts to achieve its goals. You look for ways to get involved in your company's pursuit of excellence.

Jay works for a retail furniture store. As an empowered employee, he has a strong sense of job ownership. By regularly reviewing customer complaint forms, he learned that many customers were unavailable to shop during much of the store's hours of operation. Concerned about the problem, Jay turned customer complaints into a solution. He presented a proposal to management for the store to adjust its operating hours to times that are more convenient for customers.

Jay increased his involvement by offering to implement his suggestion, which resulted in a 20 percent increase in sales. Jay's proposal marked a transition from employee to entrepreneur, and led to his being promoted to assistant store manager.

13

Owning Your Job

Sam is a phone information employee who had several ideas for improving the call-handling system. He presented his ideas in a meeting with the hope that someone would take the initiative to implement the changes.

He was certain his ideas would increase the number of calls handled and decrease the average customer wait time. Sam was disappointed when he learned that no one followed through on his ideas.

Karen is a trainer for a software company. The company trainers travel to client sites worldwide to deliver live software training sessions. While on the road, Karen came up with a training delivery idea that would save her company time and money. Her idea was for trainers to deliver client training with web-enabled software from the home office.

Karen presented her idea to the vice president of training, including a plan for implementation. She volunteered to take the lead on the project.

A person with an employee attitude is passive and reactive. Such a person may obstruct goal achievement or resist process improvements. People with an employee attitude at work perceive that their jobs belong to someone else, and

- do only what is required
- avoid responsibility
- resist change
- complain about problems
- feel stuck.

Being entrepreneurial means taking responsibility, becoming self-reliant, and showing initiative.

People with an entrepreneurial attitude at work:

- perceive that their jobs belong to them
- go the extra mile
- invite responsibility
- embrace change
- generate solutions to problems
- create meaningful work.

As you learn more about the characteristics of an employee attitude, think about someone you've noticed at work who demonstrates these characteristics. How does possessing these characteristics affect your coworker's productivity?

Perceiving That Your Job Belongs To Someone Else

A person with an employee attitude perceives that his job belongs to someone else. His perspective is that his work doesn't benefit him; only his employer profits from his effort. He has little or no sense of ownership over his job.

Do Only What Is Required

People with an employee attitude do only what is required by performing the basic duties outlined in their job descriptions. They do not seek opportunities outside the parameters of their jobs, nor do they volunteer to assist others in their efforts.

Avoid Responsibility

An individual with an employee attitude avoids responsibility by blaming others for problems that arise at work. She makes others responsible for problems or issues.

Resist Change

People with an employee attitude resist change efforts at work, especially if the change is going to affect them. Rather than embracing and facilitating change efforts, these employees obstruct, resist, and sabotage change.

Complain About Problems

Individuals with an employee attitude complain about problems instead of taking the initiative to solve them. They waste time and energy complaining about the state of a project or a company rather than channeling their energy into being part of the solution.

Feel Stuck

People with an employee attitude feel trapped in their current positions. They don't perceive that they have a choice to make a change if they are dissatisfied at work.

Have you ever heard anyone at work say something like, "The quality assurance process is so inefficient.

It just shows how incompetent the management team is. If I were in management, I would revamp the entire process"? Or maybe, "We're being asked to change the way we document our customer interactions. I thought it was better the old way. I'm going to keep doing it my way and see whether anyone notices"? These statements – and the three that follow – express an employee attitude.

- "I have no say in my job. I answer to customers, supervisors, and subordinates. I meet everyone's needs except for my own."
- "Although I know the team presentation could be better, I think it's good enough. I've already done my part."
- "My team leader would like me to lead the process improvement group because of my experience in this area, but I'm not going to volunteer. Heading up this effort would be a major headache."

Consider those you've observed at work who demonstrate the entrepreneurial characteristics. How does having these characteristics influence your coworkers' effectiveness?

Perceiving Job Belongs To You

An employee with an entrepreneurial attitude takes ownership of his job and his company. He perceives that he is partially responsible for the success or failure of the company.

Going The Extra Mile

Employees with an entrepreneurial attitude go the extra mile to achieve a goal or to complete a task or project. They are willing to put in extra time and effort, even if it requires a personal sacrifice.

Inviting Responsibility

An employee with an entrepreneurial attitude invites responsibility. If a need arises for someone to oversee a task, activity, or project component, such an employee will volunteer to take on more responsibility.

Embracing Change

Employees with an entrepreneurial attitude embrace change even if it causes discomfort. Entrepreneurial individuals realize that change is often required for improving products, processes, and profits. They offer early buy-in and contribute to change initiatives.

Generating Solutions To Problems

Employees with an entrepreneurial attitude generate solutions to problems. When problems arise, these employees identify the problems and propose solutions. They also offer to implement the solutions. Rather than complain about problems, they take action.

Creating Meaningful Work

An employee with an entrepreneurial attitude creates meaningful work wherever she is. She looks to enhance and enrich her daily work routine.

To express an **entrepreneurial attitude,** you could say something like, "I saw that a coordinated effort was required to complete our marketing portfolio. I volunteered to head up the effort." Or, "When I saw that client requests were not being dealt with, I proposed a solution for tracking all requests and volunteered to coordinate the implementation."

The following statements also reflect ways you can express your entrepreneurial attitude.

- "Meeting or exceeding my sales quota is important for the company's bottom line. Although everyone on the sales team has a quota, none of us have the same approach to selling. I've tailored my job so that it works for both me and my company."
- "The management team implemented a new team approach to client management that several of my colleagues opposed. I offered to lead a discussion outlining the benefits of the new approach."
- "The project timeline was so tight that I offered to work overtime as needed until the deadline was met."
-

To thrive in the business world, it is important to stop thinking like an employee, and start thinking and acting like an entrepreneur. Being entrepreneurial involves:

- taking on more responsibility
- becoming more self-reliant
- showing initiative.

14

Taking Initiative

"I always wondered why somebody doesn't do something about that. Then I realized I was somebody." – Lily Tomlin, actress

Initiative is taking action to accomplish a task or goal without waiting for someone else to tell you what to do. Initiative starts with the belief that you can make a difference at work. You also want to cultivate personal attributes that demonstrate initiative. The personal attributes that demonstrate initiative are:

- going above and beyond your job description
- helping coworkers successfully execute tasks
- taking risks
- seeing an activity through to completion.

Taking initiative at work is a key ingredient in making improvements, coping with change, and providing excellent customer service.

Going Above And Beyond Job Description

When you go above and beyond your job description, you look for assignments where you can make a contribution, and you volunteer to play a role.

Helping Coworkers Successfully Execute Tasks

To help coworkers successfully execute tasks, look for opportunities to assist others in meeting deadlines or in performing tasks they may be struggling with.

Taking Risks

Taking a risk is offering to perform work that allows you to move outside your normal tasks and stretch yourself professionally. Such risk taking enhances your skill sets and abilities. It's important to make sure the work is challenging but not overwhelming.

Seeing An Activity Through To Completion

When you see an activity through to completion, you take responsibility for a process from start to finish.

Employees of a risk-consulting firm are taking initiative at work. The company helps clients decrease their exposure to global threats, leverage business opportunities, and protect employees and asset services.

Oliver

Oliver, an administrative assistant, offered to organize prospective client files when he discovered vast disorganization in the marketing department. Oliver went above and beyond his job description.

George

George offered to help Sasha when he saw that she was struggling to finish her business intelligence design document, which was due to a client at the end of the day. He helped a coworker successfully execute a task.

Kathleen

Kathleen offered to deliver a client presentation on security, protection, business continuity, and emergency management when she learned that the consultant responsible for the account was ill. She took a risk; she had never before delivered a client presentation.

Amanda

Amanda made sure that each department contributed its part to the client proposal on crisis and emergency management. When she saw that the proposal was complete, she delivered it to the client. Amanda saw an activity through to completion.

The first attribute for taking initiative is going above and beyond your job description. There are two strategies for demonstrating initiative by exercising this attribute.

Propose Improvements

Keep your eyes open and look for ways to improve processes, procedures, and quality at work. Then devise and propose a plan for improvement.

Implement Improvements

Volunteer to implement the improvements yourself. It's better to do it yourself than to ask a coworker or to wait for someone else to volunteer.

Lisa is a member of a project team that is developing a web-based sales tool for a major publishing company. She was troubled by the number of bugs and errors in the prototype and thought someone should improve the quality assurance processes. She shared her ideas for quality assurance improvements, hoping that someone would use her suggestions.

How did Lisa do in demonstrating initiative by going above and beyond her job description?

Although Lisa had ideas for improving the quality assurance process, she did not volunteer to implement the improvements herself. She should have taken the lead rather than wait for someone else to volunteer.

Doug is a corporate trainer with a consulting company. Throughout his two years with the company, he noticed that the quality of the training delivery was inconsistent. Some trainers delivered flawless training sessions, while others delivered mediocre sessions. He had an idea for using videotaping and coaching sessions to improve training delivery. He proposed his idea to the director of training and offered to coordinate the initiative.

The director took him up on the idea, and three months after the implementation, participant evaluations jumped from an average of seven to an average of nine, on a scale of one through ten.

How well did Doug demonstrate initiative by going above and beyond his job description?

Doug did an excellent job in implementing both strategies. He noticed a need for improving training delivery. He then proposed the idea and offered to coordinate the effort.

The second attribute for demonstrating initiative is helping coworkers successfully execute tasks. There are three strategies for doing so.

Know Your Limitations

Know your limits and capabilities. Don't offer to help a coworker if you're already too busy. By overcommitting, you are not being fair to yourself or to your coworker.

Offer Assistance

Offer assistance to a struggling coworker. Do not wait until that person asks for help. Instead, show initiative by offering your assistance and expertise.

Provide Coaching

Ask your coworker to perform the task while you provide instruction. Don't complete the task yourself. If you do, your coworker may not learn how to perform the task. Coaching is the most effective method.

Elizabeth is an instructional designer who works for an instructional design firm. One day, she noticed that Scott, her coworker, was struggling to perform a task with the new authoring tool. Elizabeth had a light workload that day, so she offered to help Scott. She performed the task for Scott in order to expedite the process. When it came time for Scott to perform the task again, he wasn't clear about the steps. He felt frustrated, but was reluctant to ask Elizabeth for help.

How did Elizabeth do in helping Scott to successfully execute a task?

Elizabeth assessed her workload and determined that she had time to offer assistance to a struggling coworker.

However, she did not ask Scott to perform the task while she provided instruction. This left him unable to perform the task by himself later on. This type of assistance can be ineffective because it fosters dependence.

N ate and Sally work for a financial services firm. During a meeting, Nate noticed Sally having trouble using videoconferencing software. Follow along.

Nate: Sally, I noticed in the meeting that you were struggling with the videoconferencing software. I have a lot of experience working with it. In my last job, we used videoconferencing software all the time. My project is on hold, so if you'd like, I have some time to help you.

Sally: I guess my frustration during the meeting was obvious. I've never been formally trained. Here, you can sit at my computer. I'll watch over your shoulder.

Nate: Actually, I'd like you to practice using the software while I provide instruction. That way, you'll have a better understanding of how to do it yourself.

Sally: Sounds like a good plan to me. Thanks for your help, Nate.

Nate did an excellent job of helping Sally. When he saw that Sally was having trouble with the videoconferencing software, he first assessed his workload and determined that he had time to help her.

Then he offered to help her with the software. Finally, Nate insisted that Sally use the software while he walked her through the process.

To help Liza successfully execute her task, Ben should assess his work demands, and then offer to coach her on the process of completing a client needs analysis. He shouldn't overcommit himself, nor should he take over the task. If he were to overcommit, he would frustrate himself and Liza. If he were to take over the task, he would miss an opportunity to coach Lisa on the client needs analysis process.

The third attribute for demonstrating initiative is taking risks. This is an opportunity to move outside your normal tasks and stretch yourself professionally. The two strategies for taking risks are to avoid overreaching and to invite challenge.

Avoid Overreaching

Avoid taking responsibility for a task that is too far from your normal tasks.

Invite Challenge

Take on an activity that challenges you so that you gain job knowledge or learn a new skill. If the activity does not challenge you, it's not a risk.

Carla is a graphic designer who works for a web design company. Her company is launching a project with a tight timeline to create an extensive web site for a cellular telephone company. The design will include animated elements. Carla specializes in creating illustrations, static graphics, and using photographs to convey product and service offerings.

She has always been interested in learning computer animation, but has never received training in this area. Also, she has never been a lead graphic designer on a project.

Carla rethought her decision and talked to her supervisor about doing something else. She determined that it was not wise to try to teach herself computer animation while simultaneously meeting tight deadlines.

Instead, she volunteered to conceive of the overall look and feel and layout of the web site for the cellular phone company. She had never led a project before, and she felt that she could meet this challenge.

In volunteering to conceive the look and feel and layout of the web site, Carla accepted responsibility for an assignment that allowed her to move outside the comfort of her normal tasks and stretch herself professionally. This opportunity provided a challenge, but not one that would overwhelm her.

If Ben were to volunteer to lead a team in creating a public relations campaign for the software company, he would be taking responsibility for an activity that challenges him to develop leadership skills. He would be taking a risk that does not take him too far outside the comfort of his normal tasks.

If he were to volunteer to develop a media relations campaign through collaboration, he would not gain job knowledge or learn a new skill.

The fourth attribute in taking initiative is seeing an activity through to completion. Many jobs represent a single step in a long process. Some employees simply do their part and don't concern themselves with the overall perspective. To demonstrate initiative, take responsibility for creating a quality product or providing a quality service. This may also include ensuring the proper implementation of guidelines, procedures, or processes.

Follow up with your coworkers and clients to make sure the process is progressing smoothly. Remember that seeing an activity through to completion is not the same as micromanaging every step along the way.

Charlotte's firm is working on a contract that requires security compliance. Her team was given instructions about implementing the security measures, and Charlotte, as project manager, needs to make sure everyone is compliant during the project launch phase.

Which approach will best help Charlotte see this activity through to completion.

Approach 1

Charlotte plans to incorporate security measures into her job description for the duration of the project.

Approach 2

Charlotte plans to periodically check in with project team members to make sure they follow security measures.

To see the security compliance activity through to completion, Charlotte decided to adopt the second approach.

If Charlotte had simply implemented the security measures in her own job, she would not have demonstrated initiative. By following up with coworkers, she took responsibility for the proper implementation of the security compliance requirements.

To see the activity through to completion, Ben should periodically check in with the project team members and the customer to ensure adherence to environmentally sound practices.

If he were to only focus on his part of the project, Ben would not be demonstrating initiative. And if he were to monitor every step in the process, he would be micromanaging, which is inefficient and unnecessary.

If you went above and beyond your job description, helped a coworker complete her task, took a risk, and saw a support incident through to completion, you properly demonstrated to Madison that you can take initiative on projects. Demonstrating initiative will enable you to make process improvements at work and provide assistance to coworkers. It will also allow you to gain job knowledge or learn new skills, and take responsibility to ensure the proper implementation of processes or procedures.

If you did not demonstrate initiative, your team would not have a better system for capturing customer feedback. Emily might continue to struggle with customer issues. Further, you would not gain job knowledge, and you wouldn't know whether a support incident was resolved to the satisfaction of the customer.

If you find yourself wishing that someone would do something about a given problem or issue at work, remember the quote by Lily Tomlin.

Managing from Within

You are that somebody. Take initiative by going above and beyond your job description, helping coworkers successfully execute tasks, taking risks, and seeing an activity through to completion.

15

Learning Self-empowerment

Many workplace empowerment initiatives attempt to empower employees. In these initiatives, you, the employee, typically wait for your supervisor to empower you.

The problem with this model of empowerment is that no one else can empower you. That is why learning to apply a self-empowerment model is essential for managing from within.

Reflect

Take a moment to reflect on the following statement: "No one else can empower you except you." What does this statement mean to you?

An effective approach for empowering yourself is learning to apply the self-empowerment model. This model has a number of benefits.

Applying the self-empowerment model will allow you to

- enhance your feelings of self-efficacy
- assist you in assessing your performance
- help you improve your performance

- increase your sense of job mastery.

The self-empowerment model allows you to constantly monitor and improve your performance.

Self-Efficacy

Self-efficacy is the belief that you can successfully execute the behavior required to produce the desired outcome. By applying the self-empowerment model, you can set objectives and create an action plan for achieving those objectives.

Performance Assessment

Using the self-empowerment model, you can determine your current level of performance and compare it against your desired level of performance. This will enable you to assess your performance.

Performance Improvement

Once you have assessed your performance, you can create a performance improvement plan to close the gap between your desired and current levels of performance using the self-empowerment model.

Job Mastery

Monitoring and improving your performance with the self-empowerment model will increase your sense of job mastery. You will feel that your performance is on track.

Spence, a loan officer for a large bank, is a dependable professional. His supervisors consistently assigned him satisfactory ratings on his performance appraisals. Spence was concerned that such ratings would contribute to an uncertain future at the bank. Deciding that he would like to improve his lending management skills, he applied the self-empowerment model.

Enhancing Self-Efficacy

Using the model of self-empowerment, Spence set his objective – to decrease the number of bad loans made. By setting this objective, Spence enhanced his feelings of self-efficacy. He took action to address his primary performance issue.

Assessing Performance

Spence assessed his performance by evaluating how far he was from his goal. His performance metrics revealed that 5 percent of his loans were bad loans. His lack of attention to detail led to errors on those loan applications.

Improving Performance

After assessing his performance, Spence created a performance improvement plan to close the gap. He devised a system for reviewing loan applications that allowed him to catch more errors. He reduced his percentage of bad loans from 5 percent to 1 percent.

Increasing Mastery

By creating a performance improvement plan, Spence increased his job mastery. He set up a system to catch his errors that affected the quality of his loans. He felt confident that his new system would enable him to be an even more competent loan officer.

16

Understanding Self-empowerment

Do you wait for your annual performance review to receive feedback on your job performance? If you do, you're probably getting too much information, too late. To stay on top of your performance, it's important to receive feedback on a regular basis.

Self-empowered employees take the initiative to obtain the feedback they need to continuously improve their performance. They don't wait for someone else to give them the information they need to be successful in their jobs.

The self-empowerment model consists of five steps that will allow you to continuously monitor and improve your performance.

- State your objective.
- Assess the performance gap.
- Create an action plan.
- Measure the results.
- Plan for continuous improvement.

The five steps of the self-empowerment model provide a framework for setting and meeting performance improvement goals.

State Your Objective

The first step is to state your objective. Having an objective helps motivate you and allows you to follow through on your plans.

Assess The Performance Gap

The second step is to assess your performance gap. You must assess how far you are from your objective by gathering information related to the job activity in question.

Create An Action Plan

The third step is to create an action plan to achieve your objective. To close the gap between your objective and your actual performance, you must devise strategies or action items that will allow you to reach your objective.

Measure The Results

The fourth step is to measure the results of your actions by seeking concrete feedback, such as performance metrics. Performance metrics are unbiased quantitative measures of performance.

Plan For Continuous Improvement

The fifth step is to create a plan for continuous improvement by integrating your new strategies into your everyday work routine and continuing to measure your results.

Take a moment to review the five steps of the self-empowerment model.

Lucas is a technical writer with a medical instruments company who would like to decrease the number of mistakes he makes on medical instrument user manuals. He is employing the self-empowerment model to stay on top of his performance.

State His Objective

"I would like to make fewer than 50 errors per manual."

Assess The Performance Gap

"After reviewing my quality assurance reports over the past three months, I've calculated that I average 100 mistakes per manual. I'm 50 errors away from my goal."

Create An Action Plan

"I will write medical instrument user manuals while referring to the quality assurance checklist."

Measure The Results

"After using the quality assurance checklist for eight weeks, I'll assess my performance by asking the quality assurance department for performance data. If I've made fewer than 50 errors per manual during that time, I'll know I've achieved my goal."

Plan For Continuous Improvement

"I will examine my performance data every eight weeks. I plan to make the quality assurance checklist a permanent part of my work processes."

Taking a self-empowered approach to feedback and performance allows you to continuously monitor and improve your performance.

17

Managing Feedback & Performance

Applying the five steps in the self-empowerment model will allow you to take control of your performance at work.

The first step is to state your objective or desired state of affairs. To state your objective, first identify a work activity that you would like to improve. Then, state where you would like to be when you have reached your objective. Your objective should be realistic and measurable or quantifiable.

Avoid setting vague objectives that are difficult to measure. To complete this step, ask yourself, "Where would I like to be?"

Brady is a telecommunications call center representative who would like to improve his average call handling time of seven minutes. He is applying the self-empowerment model to help him achieve this objective. In the first step, he states his objective.

Incorrect

"I would like to handle customer issues more quickly."

Correct

"I would like to resolve customer issues in an average of five minutes."

In the incorrect example, Brady set an ambitious objective. If Brady were to use that objective, he would have difficulty knowing when he reached his goal.

In the correct example, Brady set a realistic and measurable objective.

He specified that he would like to resolve customer issues in an average of five minutes. He could use call center performance metrics to determine whether he achieved his objective.

The second step of the self-empowerment model is to assess your performance gap.

Your performance gap is the difference between the current state of your chosen work activity and the desired state of the activity. This gap tells you how far you are from your objective.

Brady is assessing his performance gap.

Incorrect

"I currently average seven minutes for resolving customer issues. I would like to decrease my call resolution time."

Correct

"I currently average seven minutes for resolving customer issues. I would like to average five minutes. That's a difference of two minutes."

In the incorrect example, Brady identified the current average of his call times, but he failed to compare his objective with his current state. This oversight would make it difficult for Brady to know how far he is from his current objective.

In the correct example, Brady does assess his performance gap. Assessing his performance gap lets him know how much time he must reduce from his average call time to achieve his objective.

The third step is to create an action plan for achieving your goal. An action plan consists of specific strategies or action items that enable you to close the performance gap you identified in the second step of the model. The strategies or action items you choose must specifically address the performance gap.

When completing the third step, ask yourself, "How will I improve my performance?"

For the third step, Brady creates an action plan to achieve his objective of resolving customer issues in an average of five minutes.

Comment

"I will resolve customer issues more quickly and spend less time on the phone with each customer. That will allow me to resolve customer issues in an average of five minutes."

Explanation

Brady doesn't identify specific actions that would allow him to resolve customer issues more quickly. If he were to create an action plan like this one, he would not have strategies to follow. It's unlikely that his performance would improve.

In the correct example, notice how Brady's action plan consists of specific strategies or action items that enable him to close the performance gap.

Comment

"I will create a best practices checklist for customer issue resolution. I'll use the checklist as a job aid while working with customers. The job aid will help me reach my objective of resolving customer issues in an average of five minutes."

Explanation

Brady specifies how he plans to resolve customer issues more quickly. If he uses a best practices checklist while working with customers, it's more likely that he will speed up his call resolution time.

The fourth step in the self-empowerment model is to devise an approach for measuring the results of your actions by soliciting feedback or collecting data on your performance.

If possible, seek concrete feedback or measurable performance metrics. Do this by asking yourself, "How have I improved my performance?"

To apply the fourth step, Brady, the telecommunications call center representative, plans to measure the results of his actions. Recall that his action plan is to create a best practices checklist for faster customer call resolution.

Example

"I will examine call resolution data from the project manager. I'll compare the data from before and from after I've implemented my action plan. If I've eliminated two minutes off my time for an average of five minutes per call, I'll know that I have met my objective."

Explanation

Brady outlines how he will measure the results of his actions. By examining call resolution data from before and after he carried out his action plan, he will obtain measurable performance metrics. He will be able to determine whether he has met his objective.

The fifth step is to plan for continuous improvement. To perform this step, simply repeat steps 3 and 4 – carrying out an action plan and measuring the results. Use the feedback or data from measuring your results to continuously improve your performance.

Once you have reached an objective, you may want to establish another performance objective.

To apply the fifth step, Brady plans for continuous improvement.

Incorrect

"I will examine my call resolution data once every two weeks. I'll continuously aim to improve my first-time call resolution."

Correct

"I will examine my call resolution data once every two weeks. I'll revise and use my

Managing from Within

best practices checklist until I have met my objective of five minutes per call."

In the correct example, Brady lays out his plan for continuous improvement – to carry out an action plan and measure his results. In the incorrect example, he only plans to measure his results. This will not enable him to meet his objective.

By using the model for self-empowerment effectively, you'll be able to make improvements to your presentations that will result in participant ratings of eights and nines.

If you don't apply this model correctly, you'll continue to receive satisfactory participant ratings on your presentations.

Controlling your own feedback and performance allows you to be your own best boss.

Managing from Within

Part III

Goals and Setting Goals

A well-constructed personal goal is challenging, but within your grasp. It takes into account your abilities and the resources you have available, and requires you to make the best use of both.

18

Defining Goals

In 1962, President John F. Kennedy announced the United States would embark on a program to put an astronaut on the moon. Kennedy said he chose this goal not because it was easy, but because it was hard. He said the challenge would organize and measure the best of the country's energies and skills.

Just seven years later, Neil Armstrong fulfilled Kennedy's goal when he became the first person to step onto the surface of the moon.

In the moment that Kennedy declared this audacious goal, he transformed the idea of traveling to the moon from a fantasy to an achievable ambition.

A clearly defined, attainable goal embodies a vision of what is possible. It's a guide star for developing and applying your abilities to navigate a course through obstacles to a desired destination.

Reflect

There are plenty of sources of advice about how to achieve your personal goals. However, the process of setting good goals is often overlooked. Before you begin, think about how you set goals now. What do you think makes a personal goal achievable or worthwhile?

Children dream of great but improbable futures. Some want to be a national leader, a movie star or a great sportsman. When children grow into adults, most learn there's a difference between the dreams of childhood and realistic goals.

A well-defined goal is realistic and achievable. An achievable goal is a tool to help you reach your destination. There are several benefits to defining achievable goals.

First, an achievable goal organizes and guides your work-related decisions and activities. When you strive for a clearly defined, achievable goal, you pursue decisions and activities that help you make progress in reaching that goal.

Second, achievable goals give you a way to monitor your personal progress.

As you draw nearer to reaching a goal, you can see how far you've come and how far you still have to go. You can see for yourself how much progress you've made.

Finally, goals give you a basis for communicating with others about how you perform your job.

Professional Goals

When you talk about your professional goals, you're telling others how you plan to do your job or what you've accomplished.

Personal goals

When you discuss your personal goals, you're explaining what's important to you and how you're working to change yourself.

Owen is a manager for a financial services company. Several months ago, he realized he wanted to improve his skills in interviewing job candidates. He defined an achievable goal. He made it his goal to prepare a list of questions in advance for the next five job positions for which he interviewed candidates. He also chose a mentor within his company to critique his questions.

Guiding Decisions

"My goal guided my decisions and actions. When I browsed newspapers or magazines, I chose to read articles I found about interviewing. I prepared a list of questions in advance for interviews, and I asked Susan, a human resources specialist, to critique them."

Monitoring Progress

"I measured my progress by the number of questions my mentor rejected. In the first list I compiled, she threw out six questions. When I showed her questions I'd prepared for the next open position, she only rejected two. I could see my questions were getting better."

Communicating Growth

"I discussed my goal and my progress in reaching it with my supervisor. My interest in improving my skills showed him I'm interested in the quality of job candidates we hire. Our discussions also allowed me to ask for more opportunities to use my improved skills."

An achievable goal is more than a destination. It's also a tool that helps you take the shortest path to your destination.

In this lesson, you'll explore two distinct, but interrelated types of goals you can set for yourself, and you'll examine what goes into an achievable goal.

19

Types of Goals

In some science fiction novels and movies, the future of work is bleak. Work in the future is often portrayed as dull, repetitive, and dehumanizing.

Opportunities for change, challenge, and growth make work and life more interesting and fulfilling. When writers and moviemakers want to depict a dreary future, they describe a future without these opportunities.

Your work-related goals provide opportunities for change, challenge, and growth. There are two

Goals and Setting Goals

different types of personal goals you can set to enhance your career and personal life:

- performance
- development

Performance goals set standards for results you want to achieve in your regular activities. These goals usually set targets that challenge your existing abilities and require you to stretch them to new levels of achievement.

Performance goals describe a change from your current level of performance to the targeted level and the time period in which the change will happen.

You're probably familiar with performance goals. You may have set many performance goals for yourself in your professional and personal life.

Example 1

A sales representative for a commercial printing firm sets a goal to increase sales to her current clients by $400,000 for the calendar year. She'll have to exercise her creative ability and her persuasiveness to achieve this goal.

Example 2

The assembly line manager for an automaker sets performance goals to reduce the dollar value of parts in inventory by 3 percent within 90 days. He will have to stretch his planning ability to attain the goal.

Example 3

A swimmer sets a performance goal to reduce her average time to swim 100 meters by a half second before a swim meet. She'll have to improve her strength and swimming technique to reduce her time.

Development goals describe plans to acquire new abilities or to enhance existing abilities.

These new or enhanced abilities are acquired through some type of learning activity: gaining on-the-job experience, working with a mentor, or taking an academic course or training class.

A development goal often includes a time frame for the learning activity or a deadline to give the goal urgency.

The purpose of a development goal is to expand your capabilities. In your professional life, development goals help you prepare to take on new job responsibilities. In your personal life, development goals allow you to make life more rewarding and interesting.

Example 1

An assistant buyer for a department store sets a goal to develop her skill in managing merchandise. She will gain on-the-job experience by placing orders for merchandise. She will be ready to manage her own department at the end of the year.

Example 2

An environmental engineer sets a development goal to improve his ability to lead meetings. He will receive mentoring from an experienced colleague. The colleague will review the engineer's plans for conducting five meetings and will critique the plans.

Example 3

An information systems manager sets a development goal to learn how to manage her personal finances. She will take a night class in financial management at the local community college. She will begin applying her new knowledge immediately.

Performance goals and development goals are often interrelated. A performance goal may require an associated development goal because new or enhanced skills will be needed to attain the targeted performance level.

Recall the commercial printing sales representative who set a performance goal to increase sales. She may set an accompanying development goal to take a time-management course as a tool to help her reach her sales goal.

A performance goal can also be used to help you determine whether you've successfully achieved a development goal. The department store assistant buyer set a performance goal to prepare monthly purchasing plans for eight categories of merchandise for the next three months.

She will complete the plans in the same amount of time allowed for senior buyers. If she can attain this performance goal, she will have evidence that she also attained her development goal.

Goals are a way of managing change. Without change and the challenges it brings, life would be monotonous.

Performance goals raise your aim and take full advantage your current abilities. Development goals expand your abilities and prepare you for new opportunities.

20

Setting Goals

Why do people so often fail to keep their New Year's resolutions? Many times it's because they've set goals for themselves that can't be achieved.

Achievable goals have two required components: an objective component and a standards component. A third optional component – a conditions component – may also be included to support the required components.

The objective component describes a specific activity that will be performed by the person trying to achieve the goal.

A goal must have an objective component to be achievable.

Here are several examples of activities described in objective components of goals:

- Increase sales for a service.
- Reduce costs of materials.
- Complete a course in a specific subject.
- Submit a plan for implementing a procedure.
- Write a report that describes a process.
- Teach staff to perform a task.
- Conduct interviews to gather information.

A standards component measures whether an objective has been reached. Common types of standards include a count of successful results, a degree of change, or a deadline for completion. A goal may include more than one standards component. Here are some examples of standards components:

- within six weeks
- eight times successfully
- by 30 percent
- less than five occurrences
- varying by less than 5 percent

The conditions component is any phrase that sharpens the focus of goals. Conditions components are used as needed to clarify the objective or limit the way in which it can be achieved.

Two examples of goals consisting of an objective component and a standards component are given.

Goal 1

Condition: Without increasing the number of product defects. This condition puts a limit on the effects of reducing materials cost.

Goal 2

Condition: Select staff members with the most seniority. This condition narrows the choice of which staff members can be trained to fulfill the objective.

Each of these components must be used appropriately to create an achievable goal. For instance, the objective component of an achievable goal should describe an outcome that is within the control of the goal seeker.

If achieving the goal depends on the actions or decisions of others, attaining the goal isn't entirely within your control.

The activity or result described in an objective component should be something you can observe and measure.

If you can't observe and measure the result, it will be difficult to know whether you've attained the goal.

Brian is a sales representative for a grain milling company. He worked on setting personal goals for the coming year. He's considered the listed objective components. Which of the objective components do you think are appropriate for Brian to use?

Increase Sales In The Assigned Territory

This is an appropriate objective component. Brian controls his own results by calling on customers and making convincing sales presentations. The results of those efforts can be measured by the dollar value of the products sold.

Achieve The Highest Team Sales

This is not an appropriate objective component. Brian can't control how hard other sales representatives work or what level of sales they achieve. Their actions affect whether Brian achieves the highest team sales.

Write A Report That Describes A Billing Process

This is an appropriate objective component. Brian controls how much time he spends gathering data and writing the report. He doesn't depend on anyone else to achieve the objective. The result can be observed and measured in terms of how quickly he produces the report.

Understand How The Billing Process Works

This is not an appropriate objective component. Brian's understanding of the billing process isn't something that can be observed or measured. If Brian creates an objective that demonstrates his understanding, such as writing a report, that would be an appropriate objective.

When you create a standards component for a goal, it should describe how you will measure the activity or results in your objective component. You also set a specific target – a percentage, count, or time – that you're striving to achieve.

Your standards component must also reflect realistic expectations. Your target level of achievement should challenge you to do your best, but it should also leave a little room for inevitable mistakes. Nobody's perfect.

Brian, the milling company sales representative, proposed standards components in each of his personal goals. His standards components are listed along with their related objectives. Examine each one and determine whether it's appropriate within an achievable goal.

Increase Sales In The Assigned Territory By 8% Over Last Year

This is an appropriate standards component. The objective, increasing sales, will be measured by calculating the percentage sales increase over the previous year. The target level of achievement is very specific – 8 percent.

Increase Sales In An Assigned Territory By A Significant Percentage Over Last Year

This is not an appropriate standards component. The method of measuring sales increases is adequately described – the increase will be calculated as a percentage change from the previous year. However, the target of a "significant percentage" is not specific.

Write A Report That Describes The Billing Process And Contains No Errors

This is not an appropriate standards component. Even an expert on the company's billing system may be unable to prepare a report that's entirely free of errors. This standards component sets a target for success that isn't realistic.

Within Four Weeks, Complete A Report Describing The Billing Process, And Submit It To The Supervisor

This is an appropriate standards component if Brian can realistically expect to complete his report in four weeks. This standards component measures the report writing activity in terms of how long it takes to complete. The standard for success is specific at four weeks.

Conditions components are limitations on how you achieve your objective. Use them when there are activities or results that must be included or avoided as you pursue your goal.

If some possible activities for achieving your goal will cause harm or create new problems, a conditions component limits your choices. The potentially harmful activities are specifically excluded.

Brian needs to add a conditions component to his goal to increase sales within his territory by 8 percent over last year. Two possible conditions components for this goal are given. Which of the conditions components do you think is appropriate to make his goal more achievable?

While Maintaining Current Profit Margins

This is an appropriate conditions component because it limits how Brian can achieve his sales goal. He can't make sales at a lower profit margin to increase his sales.

While Adding New Accounts

This isn't an appropriate conditions component because it doesn't narrow or clarify the objective of increasing sales. It's just an additional objective.

If you set your goals properly and include the necessary components, you'll have a better chance of success. Appropriate objective and standards components are required, and conditions components are often helpful.

21

Thinking Strategically in Goal Setting

There's more to setting a goal than simply choosing a destination you want to reach. Setting goals requires strategic thinking to help you anticipate obstacles and collaboration with people who can help you overcome those obstacles.

When you practice strategic thinking as you set goals, you gain several important benefits.

A majority of your work-related goals require participation from others in your organization. Strategic thinking helps you identify people who can help you achieve your goals so you can gain their cooperation.

Strategic thinking also helps you assess the risks in your goals more accurately. Taking on too much risk can cause you to fail to reach your goals. Taking on too little risk may mean you're not challenging yourself.

By thinking strategically about your goals, you gain a clear picture of how much risk you're assuming.

Finally, strategic thinking helps you set goals in ways that reduce wasted effort. When you apply strategic thinking in setting your goals, you're better prepared to recognize risks and potential conflicts and take steps to avoid them or cope with them.

As a result, you're less likely to spend your time on unproductive activities. When you think strategically in setting your goals, you're better able to focus on activities that help you reach your goals.

Sharon is an information systems manager for a chain of discount shoe stores. Last year she set a goal to teach store managers how to use the company's computerized inventory tracking system to send reorder requests to the central purchasing office. Sharon applied strategic thinking to improve the achievability of her goal.

Collaboration

"Our company operates more than 300 stores in 25 states. I couldn't train all of the store managers by myself. To achieve my goal, I needed to collaborate with the director of stores. Without his help, reaching my goal would have been impossible."

Risk

"I realized there was a risk that giving store managers new capabilities might conflict with the central purchasing office's goal to narrow the assortment of shoe styles in our stores. I made sure my training wouldn't conflict with that goal."

Productivity

"Thinking strategically about my goal helped me use my time productively. I developed my training session with help from the director of stores and I presented it to the central purchasing staff. These steps helped me avoid mistakes that could derail my progress."

Thinking strategically is an essential part of setting achievable goals. Without strategic thinking, you're not likely to find the most direct path to your destination.

22

Assessing Risk

The purpose of setting a goal is to gain a reward. However, striving for a goal means you must also accept the risk of failure.

Setting any work-related goal requires an investment of time and effort. If you attain your goal, your investment results in success. However, there's always a risk you'll fail to achieve a goal and your time and effort will be lost.

The amount of risk in a goal correlates to the time and effort required to achieve it. Low-risk goals usually require a small amount of investment of time and effort. High-risk goals often require a large investment of time and effort.

Both high-risk and low-risk goals are appropriate types of work-related goals. However, you probably pursue more than one goal at a time. Assessing the combined risk of all your goals can help you evaluate whether you're investing your time and effort wisely.

High Risk

If many of your goals are high-risk goals, their combined potential rewards may be very large. However, too many high-risk goals may overtax your resources.

Low Risk

If many of your goals are low risk, there's less opportunity for failure, but low-risk goals aren't as challenging and don't offer big rewards.

To assess the combined risk of all of the goals you're pursuing at any time, first classify each individual goal as high risk or low risk.

To classify each goal, you must examine how achieving your goal requires you to change conditions that exist to conditions you want. As the time and effort to create a change increases, so does the risk associated with your goal.

There are four different ways goals describe a change in existing conditions to desired conditions. Two types of change are associated with high-risk goals.

Create

Creating a new condition requires you to acquire an entirely new skill or accomplish something that hasn't been done before. The desired conditions don't yet exist, so a goal seeker is responsible for a high degree of change.

Eliminate

Eliminating an existing condition is like putting out a fire. A condition exists that needs to be ended. Elimination objectives carry a high degree of risk because they may cause unforeseen results and can disrupt the work of others.

Ron is a news producer for a television station. He has created a set of goals that he wants to accomplish in the upcoming year.

Before he can assess how much risk all of his goals represent together, he must classify each goal as high risk or low risk.

Ron set a goal to create a new weekly feature segment for his station's news program. The new feature will profile local artists and musicians. The station doesn't run any similar features, so Ron will have to plan the series, win approval, write the segments, and supervise taping.

Ron classified this as a high-risk goal because he will have to create the new series of feature segments from the beginning. He has to create a condition – airing a series of feature segments – that doesn't currently exist.

Ron also set a goal to end the need for daily noon meetings with his news production team. Ron has decided that the meetings aren't productive.

He considers this a high-risk goal because he's eliminating an existing condition – the meetings that have been held every day for many years will cease. Ron will have to make sure eliminating the meetings doesn't deprive his team members of information they need to do their jobs.

The remaining two types of change are associated with low-risk goals.

Preserve

Preserving an existing condition requires you to make marginal changes or improvements to results that have already been achieved. Preserving an existing condition is a low-risk goal because you're working to keep results that already exist.

Avoid

Avoiding an unwanted condition requires you to keep errors or other negative events from taking place. This reflects a low-risk goal because the condition you want already exists. Your goal is to avoid exceptions or changes.

Ron holds his production team to a rigid deadline. All recorded news stories are complete and ready to broadcast 20 minutes before the broadcast begins. The team was successful in meeting this deadline 96 percent of the time last year. Ron set a goal to increase that to 98 percent of the time.

This goal preserves an existing condition, so Ron considers it a low-risk goal. The condition for success – meeting the deadline – already exists. Ron only has to take steps to marginally improve that condition to achieve his goal.

One of Ron's duties as a news producer is to make sure to prepare enough news stories for a 30-minute program. Ron set a goal to provide the right amount of news content to avoid having any night's program run more than ten seconds too long or too short.

This is a low-risk goal for Ron. He has to use existing methods to avoid an unwanted condition.

To assess the combined risk in a set of goals, count the number of high-risk and low-risk goals. The combined risk is balanced between high-risk and low-risk goals if there is the same number of each type of goal.

If the number of high-risk goals exceeds the number of low-risk goals, you're aggressive in assuming risk. A difference of one goal is somewhat aggressive. A difference of two or more goals is very aggressive.

If you set more low-risk goals than high-risk goals, you're being cautious in taking on risk. A difference of just one goal indicates you're somewhat cautious. A difference of two or more is a sign you're being very cautious.

Beware of hidden or unstated goals. For example, if you're constantly struggling to cover all of your job duties or meet schedules, you probably have an unstated goal to improve your performance in those areas.

If you discover that you have unstated goals, include them in your count of high-risk goals. That will force you to be more cautious in assuming risks in your stated goals to bring their combined risk into balance.

Ron, the news producer, classified each of his goals as high risk or low risk.

He counted his goals to create a new feature segment and to eliminate mid-day meetings as high-risk goals. He counted his goals to maintain deadlines and avoid variances in the length of newscasts as low-risk goals.

As long as Ron doesn't have any unstated goals, the combined risk in his goals is balanced between high-risk and low-risk goals. However, if he recognizes that he has an unstated goal and counts it as a high-risk goal, his overall risk is somewhat aggressive.

Assessing risk is an important part of setting goals. However, there's no level of risk that's right for everyone. It's up to you to decide how much risk you're willing to accept to achieve your goals.

23

Collaborating on Goals

Some goals may seem too hard to achieve on your own.

When you need help to achieve a goal, that's a good time to find a partner with whom you can collaborate.

The people who can help you achieve your goals won't always share your goals. Their goals may even conflict with yours. You can resolve conflicts and build partnerships by applying these steps to create a collaborative goal:

- Define the conflict.
- Propose a collaboration.
- Define collaborative roles.

The first step in creating a collaborative goal is defining conflicts between your goals and the goals of another member of your organization.

Describe your own goal in terms of what you need to accomplish. Then ask the other person to describe the need she seeks to fulfill by achieving her conflicting goal.

Defining conflicting goals is an information-gathering step. Use this step to learn as much as you can about the other person's goal.

Define the conflict by learning what the other person needs to accomplish. This helps you avoid making the conflict personal. A conflicting goal isn't a personal attack. It's an opportunity for innovation and collaboration.

If you focus on what you need and what Dwight needs, the conflict between your goals and his is less likely to become a personal conflict. Discussing needs gives Dwight an opportunity to help you.

The next step in creating a collaborative goal is to propose the collaboration. Propose a single goal that addresses your own needs as well as the needs of the other party. Make your suggestion and ask for the other person's opinion.

Resist the urge to seek an advantage over the person who holds the conflicting goal. Don't try to argue that your goal is more important or more urgent. Respect your coworker's right to pursue goals of her own.

Proposing a collaboration isn't the same as suggesting a compromise. When two people with conflicting goals compromise, neither gets what he wants.

A collaborative goal creates a way for both parties to achieve their goals.

Dwight responded favorably to a proposed collaborative goal. Why wouldn't he? The collaborative goal gives him help in achieving his own goals.

The final step in creating a collaborative goal is to define roles for the participants in the collaboration.

The roles for the participants should be equal. Neither participant should assume authority over the other. Both participants should contribute equal amounts of effort and receive equal benefit.

Collaboration means working together. The roles for the participants in a collaborative goal should begin at the same time and involve as many shared activities as possible. When you propose roles, clearly define what both parties will contribute. If you don't, you haven't created a real collaboration.

Avoid proposing a collaboration that requires one participant to complete her share of the work before the other participant begins. That may create a perception that one participant is allowed to delay his work until later.

Your strategy for creating a collaborative goal won Dwight as a partner in achieving your goal. He's no longer an obstacle. He's a member of your team.

If you applied the three steps correctly, you resolved the conflict between Dwight's need to hold down payroll costs and your need to increase the number of hours worked by call center operators.

With strategic collaboration, the person who seems to be an obstacle in your path can become an ally, a partner in attaining your goal.

24

Aligning Priorities and Goals

There's a big difference between a goal and an accomplishment. Setting a goal is the beginning of a process. If you're successful, an accomplishment comes at the end of the process.

There are several benefits that come from aligning your priorities and your goals. When your priorities accurately reflect your goals, you're more likely to get started and do what's needed to achieve important or urgent goals. You're less likely to procrastinate or to delay in taking action.

Prioritizing actions that will help you achieve your goals leads to another benefit: you achieve goals more quickly. When your priorities align with your goals, you don't have to wait as long to realize the rewards of your work.

Keeping your priorities and goals aligned also helps you recognize when it's time to let go of a goal. If your goal no longer seems to be worth a top-priority effort, it's time to reassess your priorities or set an alternative goal.

Roberta is a marketing manager for a consumer products company. She set a goal to develop her listening skills and she succeeded. She believes that aligning her priorities with that goal made the difference.

Explanation 1

"When I set a goal to improve my listening skills, I made that goal one of my top priorities. When I found a self-study course on the subject, I took it right away."

Explanation 2

"Improving my listening skills has been something I've been meaning to do for years. Once I aligned my priorities with that goal, I achieved it in just a couple of months."

Roberta had originally wanted to develop her listening skills by attending a three-day seminar led by a popular author and psychologist. However, she could never find the time in her schedule – or the money to pay the expensive tuition fee – when the seminar was being offered.

When she aligned her priorities with her goal, she realized it was time to let go of her original plan and find an alternative.

Aligning your priorities and goals is a valuable tool in your goal-setting process.

In this lesson, you'll examine how to compare your goals against each other and prioritize each one.

You'll also explore strategies for choosing alternative goals when your progress is blocked. You'll learn how to preserve what was important in your original goal while choosing a new path to achieve it.

25

Prioritizing Goals

Few people enjoy the luxury of pursuing only one goal at a time.

Most have to juggle several goals simultaneously.

When you pursue several goals at once, you have to prioritize some goals ahead of others. There are two elements that determine the priority you assign to any goal:

- the importance or value of achieving the goal
- the availability of resources needed to reach the goal

The potential rewards you and your organization receive for achieving a goal determine the importance or value of the goal. There are two factors to consider when you evaluate the importance of a goal – personal importance and professional importance.

Personal Importance

A goal has a high level of personal importance when achieving the goal satisfies your own values or desires. It means that achieving the goal matters to you.

Professional Importance

A goal has professional importance when achieving it satisfies the duties or requirements of your job. It means achieving the goal matters to your employer.

Warren is an account representative for a company that sells employee identification systems. He set several goals for the coming year. His goals don't have the same level of importance.

Update Customer Contact Information In The Company Sales Database.

"This goal is moderately important to me personally. Organizing contact information makes calling on clients easier. It's also personally satisfying to me. This goal has low professional importance, though. My boss doesn't care how well I maintain my contact database."

Perform At Least Ten Sales Presentations To Potential New Clients Within 120 Days.

"This goal has a low level of personal importance for me. I don't enjoy giving presentations to potential clients. I prefer working with established accounts. However, this goal has high professional importance. I'm evaluated on the number of presentations I give."

Prepare A Training Presentation To Help New Customers Use The Company's Identification System Effectively.

"This goal has a high level of personal importance for me. I like to teach new clients how to make the most of our company's products. This goal also has a high level of professional importance. My boss expects me to train new clients and win their trust."

The priority you assign to a goal should be determined by the availability of resources you can apply to achieving it. There are two factors to consider about resource availability: resource readiness and resource urgency.

Select the two factors to consider about resource availability to learn more about them.

Resource Readiness

Resource readiness is the amount of time, money, materials, or knowledge ready to be applied. You're able to act more quickly when resources are available.

Resource Urgency

The urgency of resources is how quickly resources must be used. If a deadline is approaching or a key team member will soon become unavailable, urgency is high.

Warren, the sales representative for the identification systems company, evaluated the readiness and urgency of resources he could apply to his three goals.

Update Customer Contact Information In Company Sales Database.

"This goal has a low level of resource readiness. I need at least one full day to perform this task, but my schedule is full. The urgency to perform this task is low. I can afford to postpone organizing my client contact information. There's no deadline for getting it done."

Perform At Least Ten Sales Presentations To Potential Clients Within 120 Days.

"This goal has a very low level of resource readiness. I don't have the required knowledge to perform these presentations. The person who can help me is out of town for a month. However, the urgency to complete this goal is growing. The time to my deadline is growing short."

Prepare Training Presentation To Help New Customers Use The Company's Identification System Effectively.

"This goal has a high level of resource readiness. I have the time I need to work on this task and a training specialist has been assigned to me. The urgency for this goal is moderate. I may have plenty of time, but the training specialist won't be available after next week."

To prioritize a set of goals, you must weigh the importance and resource availability to be applied for each one. Then compare each goal to all the others.

First, rate each goal on a scale of 1 to 5 for personal importance and professional importance. Assign a value of 1 to goals with relatively low importance. Assign a value of 5 to very important goals.

Add the values for personal importance and professional importance together to obtain a total value for the importance of each goal.

Calculate an importance value for all of the goals that must be prioritized. The results will all fall between 2 for the least important goals and 10 for the most important goals.

Perform the same process for resource readiness and resource urgency. Assign a value between 1 and 5 for each criterion.

Assign low values to goals for which resources aren't readily available and for which urgency is low. Assign high values to goals where plenty of resources are readily available and the urgency to act is high. Add the two values together.

Calculate a resource availability value for all of the goals to be prioritized. The total for each goal will fall between 2 for the goals with the lowest resource availability and 10 for the goals with the highest resource availability.

Plot the values for each goal on a priorities matrix. The vertical scale represents the importance. The horizontal scale represents the resource availability.

The position of the goals on the priorities matrix gives you an indication of the priority you should set for each one. Divide the matrix into four zones as shown. Place the dividing lines between zones 5 and 6 on both the vertical and horizontal scales.

Zone 1

Goals that fall in zone 1 are top priorities. They have a high level of importance and resources are available. You should act immediately to achieve these goals.

Zone 2

Goals in zone 2 can be delayed until later but must be watched carefully. These goals have a high level of importance, but resources aren't available or there isn't an urgent need to act. A change in resource availability could raise the priority of these goals.

Zone 4

Goals in zone 4 aren't important and resources aren't available. You may consider abandoning these goals.

Zone 3

Goals in zone 3 should be reconsidered or reformulated. Although resources are available, these goals don't have a high level of importance. Until they become more meaningful, there's no hurry to act on these goals.

Warren, the account representative, created a list of goals he wanted to pursue. His list is shown above.

He rated each of his goals for resource readiness and for urgency. He added the ratings together to obtain a total rating for resource availability.

Warren rated each goal for personal and professional importance. He added the ratings for each goal together to obtain an overall importance rating.

Warren used a priorities matrix to prioritize his goals. He used the resource availability rating and the importance rating to place a data point for each goal on the matrix. Warren used the location of the data points to determine the priority of each goal.

3

This data point represents Warren's goal to prepare training for new clients. He rated this goal 7 for resource availability and 9 for importance. The data point for this goal is in zone 1, so Warren should make it a top priority.

2

This data point represents Warren's goal to perform ten new sales presentations. This goal has a resource availability rating of 4 and an importance rating of 7. This data point is in zone 2. Warren can delay acting on this goal, but he should watch for changes.

5

This data point represents Warren's goal to receive mentoring. He gave this goal a total resource availability rating of 5 and an importance rating of 7, so it falls in zone 2. Warren can delay acting on this goal, but he should watch for changes.

4

This data point represents Warren's goal to perform a return-on-investment analysis. He gave this goal a rating of 7 for resource availability and a rating of 8 for importance. The data point is in zone 1, so Warren should make this goal a top priority.

1

This data point represents Warren's goal to organize his client contact file. He gave this goal a rating of 4 for resource availability and a rating of 4 for importance. Because the data point for this goal is in zone 4, Warren should consider abandoning it.

When Warren plotted his goals on a priorities matrix, the goals that were most important and most achievable became apparent. He applied his immediate efforts to achieving those goals.

However, he didn't neglect the rest. He made conscious decisions about delaying, reconsidering, or abandoning the others.

26

Setting Alternative Goals

There will be times when you can't achieve some of your goals. That's when it's time to consider alternative goals.

Reflect

If you achieve all of the goals you set, you're not challenging yourself enough. When your goals are challenging, some of them will turn out to be unattainable. What strategies do you use when you realize that one of your goals may be unattainable?

You don't have to give up on a goal just because it doesn't work out the way you expected. Persistence will result in success. You can set an alternative goal using one of these three strategies:

- breaking out smaller objectives
- reassessing priorities
- seeking a different path to the destination

The first strategy for setting alternative goals is breaking out smaller objectives. When a larger objective can't be obtained within the standard you've set, breaking out a smaller objective allows you to be partially successful.

To break out a smaller objective, see if there's a portion of your original goal that can be achieved separately. Narrow the effect of your goal on fewer people or events. You can always address the remainder of your original goal later.

Vicki is a broker for a financial services firm. She set a goal to increase her sales by 12 percent. Her original strategy was to find 20 new clients by the end of the year. Her original goal now seems too challenging, so Vicki is considering alternative goals.

Smaller Goal

Vicki can limit her goal to a single product line, like life insurance or retirement accounts. Achieving a 12 percent increase in a limited area will be a partial success.

New Goal

Vicki can create a new goal to increase her sales in other product lines later. That will allow her to achieve her original goal.

The second strategy for setting alternative goals is reassessing priorities. Another look at the importance and resources associated with a goal may reveal changes in either or both elements of the goal's priority.

Don't be afraid to postpone dealing with one goal in order to pursue a goal that has become more important. You can return to your original goal later if changing conditions make it important again.

Vicki, the financial services company broker, had set a goal to receive mentoring on closing sales from her sales team leader.

However, her sales team leader couldn't make time to provide the training. Vicki reassessed the priority of receiving mentoring.

The resources Vicki needed to develop her sales closing skills weren't available.

She decided she could delay working on that skill.

With her sales team leader's advice, she decided to make developing her knowledge of the company's products a higher priority.

The third strategy for setting alternative goals is choosing a different path. There's more than one way to reach most destinations. If you can't develop or improve skills through education, you can choose on-the-job experience, or find a mentor instead.

You can improve profitability by increasing sales or by reducing costs. You can save time by doing work more quickly or by eliminating unnecessary work. Choosing a different path allows you to take an alternate route to your objective.

Vicki could choose to take a different path to achieve her goal of a 12 percent sales increase.

New Customers

Vicki's original strategy was to find 20 new clients. Her sales to new clients would provide the increase in sales to achieve her goal.

Existing Customers

Instead of seeking 20 new clients, Vicki chose to focus on her existing clients. She set up meetings with her ten largest clients to show them additional products her company offers.

There are a couple of common strategies you shouldn't use when you need an alternative goal. Relaxing the standard for your goal isn't a good strategy. Extending your deadline or reducing the amount of change you expect to achieve is just lowering the standard for success, not setting an alternative goal.

Ignoring the conditions on your original goal is also not a good strategy. Conditions limit how you go about achieving a goal to prevent unwanted or unexpected results. Ignoring them may make achieving your goal more costly.

Goals should be reassessed and reworked continuously. Knowing how to set alternative goals gives you a way to try, try again if at first you don't succeed.

Part IV

A Positive Attitude

Having a positive attitude means being realistic about your situation and why things are happening, and trying to find a way to capitalize on your experiences – positive and negative – instead of allowing them to grind you down.

27

Changing Your Perspective

How's it going?

The way you react to this question reveals a lot about you – and your attitude.

Perception is the physical sensation interpreted in the light of experience; perspective is the way you see or look at something; attitude is the mental position, feeling, or emotion toward a fact or state.

All of these influence the way you interact with the world around you. So all of these will also impact your ability to be positive or negative in any given situation.

Your attitude toward your work, your job, and the situations you find yourself in has a significant impact on how effective, productive, and happy you are. If you have a positive attitude, you're more likely to succeed than if you have a negative attitude.

But why is this?

If you have a negative attitude, you feel bad about the things that happen to you, and you expect the worst.

As a result, when bad things happen, you feel bad, and you're trapped in a cycle of negativity.

Conversely, if you have a positive attitude, you generally feel good about your situation, and so when bad things happen you can take them in stride as "one of those things," and move on.

_____

Having a positive attitude isn't about being blindly optimistic. Things go wrong sometimes, and pretending that things will "be OK in the end" is not a good way to manage your life.

Having a positive attitude means being realistic about your situation and why things are happening, and trying to find a way to capitalize on your experiences – positive and negative – instead of allowing them to grind you down.

Have you ever noticed how some people can see something good in every situation?

One of the best ways to do this is to alter the way you look at the situations you find yourself in. Positive people always look at things from a positive perspective.

You may be lucky enough to have a "sunny disposition," but most people find themselves looking at the negative side of situations at some point.

If you can look at what happens to you from a positive perspective, then you can deal with situations positively.

Changing your perspective from negative to positive can benefit you by:

- enabling you to take control of what happens to you
- letting you examine your reactions so that you don't overreact to situations
- allowing you to think of creative ways to deal with negative situations that you face.

Developing a positive attitude means taking a positive stance when faced with a situation, instead of

A Positive Attitude

withdrawing or focusing on the negative aspects of a situation.

Your ability to do this is governed by your perspective on a situation. If you can look at things from a positive standpoint instead of a negative one, you can take positive steps to deal with the issues you face.

Before you change your perspective, you need to understand what your current perspective is.

The best way to do this is to consider three aspects of any situation: what or who you believe to be in control of the situation, the extent to which your reactions are rational, and whether you focus on the negative or positive aspects of a situation.

This lesson helps you to understand what your perspective is, how it impacts your reactions, and how you can change your perspective so that you can develop a positive attitude.

"Always look on the bright side" may sound like stereotyped advice from someone who doesn't understand how difficult your situation is.

But if you do change your perspective to be positive, then you'll find that you can avoid overreacting to the situations that you face, take control of what happens to you, and find creative ways of dealing with adversity.

28

Understanding Locus of Control

Who is in control of your life?

Reflect

Do you believe you have the ability to shape events around you, or do you believe your life is in the hands of fate? Think about the last time something went wrong for you. Why did it happen?

The locus of control concept was proposed by the psychologist Julian Rotter in 1966.

The locus of control refers to what individuals believe is the controlling force behind the events that happen to them. It can be described as either internal or external.

Individuals with an **internal** locus of control are likely to believe that events result from their own behaviors and actions.

Responsibility

Individuals with an internal locus of control are willing to take responsibility for their own actions, and for what happens to them.

Positive Attitude

Individuals with an internal locus of control generally have a positive attitude because they feel they can have an impact on their own lives.

Follow along as Danny, an account executive, explains what has happened to him at work over the past few weeks.

I knew my boss was right when she criticized my handling of the Adams account in my appraisal. I had the opportunity to win the business, but I just didn't go that extra mile.

If I worked a little harder, I would have gotten the account and met my targets for the month. I'll know better next time.

I know that in the long term, I'll be able to meet my targets and my boss will respect the work that I've put in. The only person who can help me succeed is me, so I need to focus hard and get the job done.

Individuals with an **external** locus of control believe that chance, luck, or powerful people determine events.

Individuals with an external locus of control may have a tendency to distance themselves from events and their consequences, blaming others, fate, or the situation for what is happening, instead of taking responsibility for themselves.

As a result, individuals with an external locus of control often fail to have positive attitudes because they feel paralyzed and unable to act to change what is happening to them.

Patty is a colleague of Danny's, and she has also recently had an appraisal with her boss. Follow along as Patty describes what has happened to her.

My boss just doesn't understand how hard I'm working. If she doesn't realize how much effort I'm putting in, then there's nothing I can do.

Channeling Your Inner Boss   155

It's not my fault if the customers don't want to buy; it's just one of those things. There's nothing I can do about it.

If I had the right breaks, I'd easily meet my targets. It's just a matter of being in the right place at the right time. One day I'll have some luck – then my boss will realize what a great account executive I am.

Danny and Patty reacted very differently to their appraisals. Why was that?

Patty

Patty has a high external locus of control. She believes that luck will help her achieve her targets and that what her customers decide to do is outside of her control. She distances herself from her failures and doesn't take responsibility for her actions.

Danny

Danny has a high internal locus of control. He believes he's responsible for what happens to him, and as a result, he feels he can improve his performance and achieve his targets in the future.

Awareness of your locus of control can help you develop a positive attitude.

If your locus of control is external, you need to take steps to take responsibility for what happens to you, and to believe that you can positively influence your own destiny.

A Positive Attitude

If you have an internal locus of control, you take responsibility for your actions; however, it may also be good to remind yourself that sometimes it's important to take external factors into account.

The novelist John Oliver Hobbes once said, "Men heap together the mistakes of their lives, and create a monster they call destiny."

Don't let an external locus of control become the monster that stops you from achieving what you're capable of. Challenge your perspective on what happens to you, and take action to develop a more positive outlook.

29

Reacting Rationally to Events

In the Shakespeare play Hamlet, the Prince of Denmark said:

"There's nothing either good or bad, but thinking makes it so."

How you think about something influences how you feel about it. Your feelings then influence how you behave in response.

If your internal response to the events that happen to you is rational, then you can avoid the negative side effects that result from unrealistic or unfounded expectations and doubts. But what is the difference between rational and irrational internal responses?

Rational

Rational perceptions are those that are based on realistic beliefs about events. In most cases, the most likely explanation for events is the true explanation.

Irrational

Irrational perceptions are those based on unrealistic beliefs about events. People aren't usually devious and underhanded; believing so is unrealistic and irrational.

Albert Ellis, a pioneer of cognitive therapy, devised the ABC model for emotional disturbance and change. The ABC model comprises three distinct elements:

- A stands for an actual event and represents what happens to you.
- B stands for a belief about what happened.
- C stands for the consequences of the event on mood and behavior.

Harry is the supervisor of a telephone customer service team. Harry needs to change the office layout to make space for two new employees and some new printing and photocopying equipment, and to comply with his organization's new guidelines for workspaces.

Here are the choices Harry made about who should be located where, and why.

Jason

Jason is relatively new to the team, so Harry decides to place Jason's desk close to his office and right next to Arthur, one of the most experienced members of the team. This way, Jason can easily ask for help from either Arthur or Harry whenever he needs it.

Joan

Joan acts as Harry's personal assistant and also deals with customers. Harry locates Joan's desk just outside his office and close to the printing and photocopying equipment. This way, she can contact Harry easily, but she also has access to the equipment she needs.

Lillian

Lillian is one of three technical specialists who deal with technical queries. Harry decides to locate one technical specialist within each group of workspaces so that technical advice is always available to other employees. As a result, Lillian is relocated to a desk next to the window.

Arthur

Arthur is the most experienced member of the team, and he often mentors new employees. Harry relocates Arthur from his isolated workspace next to the window to a new workspace close to his office. From here, Arthur can better support the new hires.

Each member of Harry's team responds differently to the choices he made.

Jason

Jason believes his desk has been located between Harry and Arthur because he isn't trusted, and so he leaves the meeting angry when the office layout is revealed.

Joan

Joan understands that, because of her dual role as Harry's personal assistant and customer service assistant, she needs to be close to Harry and the printing and photocopying equipment. She doesn't particularly like her new workspace, but she isn't upset to have been moved.

Lillian

Although Lillian is pleased to be next to the window, she believes Harry deliberately moved her away from her friends on the technical team because she talks to them too much, and so she reacts by sulking.

Arthur

Arthur knows his old location was isolated, but he really liked being by the window. Last week, Arthur disagreed with Harry about how to deal with a difficult client, and now he feels as though Harry is punishing him by moving him.

Jason, Arthur, and Lillian all responded irrationally to the office layout because they believed Harry's motives were personal, unfair, or prejudiced.

In fact, if they had thought about what Harry was trying to achieve, they would each have seen that Harry was just trying to make the team work as effectively as possible – and their reactions would have been rational.

Joan responded rationally. She understood why Harry needed to make the changes to the office layout, so she was the only team member able to have a positive attitude about the changes.

Oftentimes, your negative feelings about what happens to you are a direct result of the way you perceive events. Stand back, try not to take things personally, and see what happens.

Reacting rationally to the events you encounter is a good way to develop a positive attitude.

30

Creating New Perspectives

John W. Gardner, the former Secretary of Health, Education, and Welfare, once said, "We are continually faced with a series of great opportunities brilliantly disguised as insoluble problems."

The idea that opportunities are disguised as problems demonstrates how, by looking at a situation in a different way, you can see new possibilities.

Creating new perspectives, or frames, can help you think beyond your own experiences and look at things in new and more positive ways.

But what kind of perspectives should you consider?

The key to using frames is to focus on the positive perspectives, not the negative ones. There are four main pairs of frames:

- problem and learning
- detail and overall
- personal and team
- conflict and negotiation

The problem frame is a negative frame in which every issue is seen as a problem. Conversely, the learning frame is a positive frame in which everything is seen as a learning opportunity.

By switching your perspective from seeing negative problems to seeing positive learning opportunities, you can begin to see the good in situations that, at first glance, appear to be disastrous.

Danny and Patty are account executives for a large public relations firm. They recently worked on a project for a pharmaceutical company. Unfortunately, the firm missed a few key deadlines, and the client was angry.

Danny

Danny used the situation to revise his project plan template so key deadlines were tracked. He also created a new procedure for managing suppliers and contracts.

Patty

Patty saw the situation as hopeless. She assumed the relationship with the client had been irrevocably broken and that she would be removed from the account.

The detail and overall pair of frames is useful when you need to be able to step back from a situation, and view it from a broader perspective. In the detail frame, the focus is on a single element of an issue, whereas in the overall frame, the focus is on an entire issue, rather than one element.

Find out how Tim, a project manager, and Mary, a chef, each switched from the detail frame to the overall frame to look at events in a positive way.

Tim's Detail

"I was panicking because our quality assurance procedures were quite cumbersome, and following them would mean the project wouldn't be completed on time."

Tim's Overall

"Then I stepped back and analyzed the project as a whole. I realized that simply deleting a couple of steps from the quality assurance process would allow us to meet our deadline without affecting the entire project."

Mary's Detail

"I was catering a wedding reception. I wanted to use Scottish oysters, but I could only get French ones. It worried me because I think the Scottish oysters are better quality."

Mary's Overall

"It suddenly occurred to me that my opinion didn't matter. The guests wouldn't care whether I served Scottish or French oysters; they would be focused on enjoying the happy occasion."

The personal and team frame pair can be very useful when used together with the detail and overall frames.

A Positive Attitude

- In the personal frame, an individual focuses only on what is happening to him instead of how events impact on others, the project, or the organization as a whole.
- In the team frame, the individual focuses on how events affect the team or organization as a whole rather than how they affect him.

Tim and Mary have both found that by switching from the personal to the team frame, they have been able to react more positively to what is happening to them. Specifically, using these frames can help you to remove yourself from the center of a situation and see what is really happening.

Find out how Tim and Mary switched from the personal frame to the team frame so they now look at events in a positive way.

Tim

"I'd finished my deadline and was looking forward to a couple of easy workdays before the next project hit. Then I realized that other team members needed help finishing their tasks or we would miss the project deadline, so I volunteered to pitch in."

Mary

"With the wedding only a week away, I felt like all the pressure was on me, and I was being pretty difficult to work with. Then I recognized that we were all feeling the pressure. I resolved to shift my focus to the wedding and what we had to do to make it successful."

The final pair of frames, conflict and negotiation, is also linked closely to the other pairs of frames. This is because the conflict frame is a negative frame in which the focus of the issue is disagreement and winning, rather than resolution and compromise.

This often means that personal issues overshadow what is good for the team or the organization.

The negotiation frame is a positive frame in which the focus is on conflict resolution and compromise.

Switching to this frame often results in a refocusing on the positive overall and team frames.

O liver and his colleague Jim can't agree on the best way to approach a technical problem on their building project. Follow along as they discuss what is happening.

Oliver: As I see it, we can fix this if your guys dig another foot down so that we can add more concrete. We could add steelwork but that would be too costly. You'll just have to do it.

Jim: Well, we wouldn't have this problem if you'd specified the concrete properly. I don't see why my team should have to work longer just because you made an error in your calculations.
Jim says defensively.

Oliver: OK. This is getting us nowhere. We're not going to agree on why we're in this position, but what

A Positive Attitude

we can agree on is that we have to move forward. How can we work together?

Oliver acknowledges.

Jim: I guess we could compromise. I can get my team to start digging now, and we'll see how far we get by close of business. Then we can look again.

Jim compromises.

Reframing or looking at things from positive perspectives will enable you to overcome your negative thoughts and feelings. It will also help you discover new ways of approaching situations that might have overwhelmed you in the past.

Where some people see problems, others see opportunities.

Looking at situations from a positive perspective is a good way of turning your problems into opportunities, and a way of making sure that you get the best out of the situations you face.

31

Changing Your Coping Skills

It's one thing to try to develop a positive perspective on the things that happen to you, but how will you cope when faced with people and situations that make you feel negative?

Coping starts with taking action to catch yourself before negative feelings take over.

Do things that help you minimize your negativity, and if necessary, challenge difficult people and situations so that you can sustain a positive outlook.

Changing your coping skills to react positively to situations can help you:

- base your reactions on facts
- improve your performance
- set boundaries and avoid feelings of frustration and being taken advantage of.

Patty works as an account executive and has a reputation for being negative. Recently, however, Patty has been working hard to change her coping skills so that she can handle negative situations better.

Before

"Looking back to my appraisal, I thought my boss was criticizing me because she didn't like me, and I felt that I was being given the most difficult clients and the least interesting jobs deliberately. I felt so miserable because I was negative about everything."

After

"I get the clients I get because that's just how things work out – I was overreacting before. I've used the feedback I've been given to improve my performance, and I realize that I'm not being taken advantage of –

we're all treated equally. I feel much more positive now."

Comic artist Tom K. Ryan once said "I will cope with adversity in my traditional manner...sulking and nausea."

A better strategy is to turn adversity to your benefit by developing techniques to cope and overcome the problems you face. As a result, you'll benefit from the positive outcomes that result from a positive attitude.

32

Challenging Negative Thinking

Do you ever hear a little voice inside your head, criticizing and undermining you?

The language that voice uses reflects the nature of your thoughts and beliefs.

If you can change it to a supportive voice, you'll be on the way to having a positive attitude.

The voice inside your head can direct the way you think and behave.

Negative Thinking

Negative thinking undermines you and makes you believe that you can't succeed.

Positive Thinking

Positive thinking gives you the confidence to take up new challenges and to believe that you can succeed.

By changing negative thoughts to positive ones, you'll find that you can manage your responses to events, and react more rationally.

Broadly speaking, there are five distinct areas of negative thoughts that need to be overcome.

Focusing On The Negative

Focusing on the negative involves selecting a single negative aspect of an experience and focusing entirely on that. Focusing on the negative can also involve dismissing and devaluing positive experiences by putting any successes down to luck.

All Or Nothing Thinking

All or nothing thinking involves looking at things in black and white terms – everything was good or everything was bad. Often, all or nothing thinking will involve misreading people's reactions or overdramatizing the importance of a minor problem.

Overgeneralization And Labeling

When you engage in overgeneralization, you see a single negative event as a never-ending pattern of defeat. In its most extreme form, it involves attaching a negative label, such as idiot or failure, to yourself or others.

Jumping To Conclusions

Jumping to conclusions is also known as "mind reading" and "fortune-telling," and it involves imagining unrealistic negative outcomes or consequences of an event.

Blame

Blame happens when you hold someone or something else entirely responsible for an event. Oftentimes, it involves an "I told you so" attitude.

Tim is a project manager who has managed the design of a major line of toys. Tim has just presented his team's designs to the client, and although the client liked most of the ideas, they requested a minor change to one of the toy's colors.

Negative Focus

"How could we have been so off on that color? It isn't what they wanted; they'd asked for a different shade of blue. We were lucky they liked the designs."

All Or Nothing

"What a disaster. The color was wrong, so I guess it's back to the drawing board. We spent so much time on this project, and they hated it."

The meeting with the client wasn't Tim's only negative experience. There have been problems with some of the suppliers, and the marketing department has just told him they're having difficulty booking media space for the launch. Can things get any worse for Tim?

Overgeneralization And Labeling

"I'm such an idiot. This always happens to me. Every time I get involved in a major project, things go wrong."

Jumping To Conclusions

"That's just great. No media space means no launch. No launch means that the client will ditch us, and I'll be fired."

Blame

"I said at the beginning of this project that we'd have problems with the suppliers but I wasn't listened to. Now marketing has let us down just like I thought they would. How can I get things done when I'm always being let down."

So how can you overcome these negative thoughts?
You can apply four simple techniques to help you. You may find that you need to use all four techniques, or you might find that one of them works well for you.

The techniques are examining the evidence, befriending yourself, putting things in context, and looking for the positive.

Underpinning all of these techniques is a need to challenge your negative thinking.

Negative self-talk usually involves exaggeration of the negative, or imagining the worst. You need to look for the actual evidence of what happened rather than simply assuming that your version of the events is the correct one.

Examining the evidence relies on you knowing what happened and not relying on your perceptions – get feedback from trusted colleagues, review a report or schedule again, or go over feedback one more time. Examining the evidence is especially useful if you tend to jump to conclusions or engage in all or nothing thinking.

Jumping To Conclusions

Challenge your assumptions – why should everything go wrong? Are things as bad as you think?

All Or Nothing

Not everything happens in black and white. Look at the elements of the event or problem – did some things go better than others, or did everything really go wrong?

Marcie, an events planner, often indulges in negative self-talk and is trying to challenge her thinking. Follow along to find out what her internal voice is saying.

You know, that sales conference was a complete disaster. Everyone was really unhappy with the food the hotel served, and no one enjoyed the main speaker.

Then again, when I asked Dana what she thought, she said the food was good. She also said that although the main speaker wasn't excellent, he made some good points.

I'm organizing another conference next month – I guess that'll be as bad as this one. We've hired a different speaker, but he'll probably be awful. And people are bound to complain about the food again.

Hold on. Why should the conference next month go badly? I've prepared for it, it's at a different hotel, and there's a different speaker. Do I have any reason to believe the food will be bad? When we've used this hotel before, it's always been excellent. I don't need to worry.

Marcie did a great job of challenging her negative thinking by examining the evidence. She started with all or nothing thinking, but then thought about what had really happened and challenged her perceptions by thinking about what Dana said.

When she found herself jumping to conclusions about the next conference, she checked herself by challenging those assumptions and looking for evidence to support them.

Negative thinking turns you into your own worst enemy. Instead of beating yourself up, think about how you would react to a friend in a similar situation.

A Positive Attitude

- What would you say?
- Would you be as harsh and judgmental as you're being to yourself?

Marcie's latest problem is a result of her ordering the wrong limousine to pick up her boss from the airport. Any of the techniques for challenging negative thinking will work in this situation, but befriending yourself is particularly effective.

First Thoughts

"I'm such a failure. Everything I do goes wrong. It was the wrong limousine today, and tomorrow I'll get the travel arrangements wrong – it'll just go downhill from there. I can't do anything right."

Befriending Herself

"When Charlie messed up the limousine rental the other week, we didn't fire him or anything. We just reminded him which car the boss likes, and that was it. Charlie wasn't fired, and there's no reason why my boss should fire me either."

Putting things in context is a very straightforward technique to use, and it can help you dismiss some of your most extreme negative thoughts. It can also help you see the extent to which you're exaggerating the problems that you face. Asking yourself these questions will put your negative thoughts into context:

- Is what's happening a matter of life and death?
- What's the worst realistic outcome?
- How bad will it seem in a day, a week, or a month?
- Will I or anyone else remember this in time?

First the conference, then the limousine. Marcie's finding it hard to challenge her negative thinking. Follow along as she tries to put things in context.

> "I can't believe things are going so badly for me. I just can't get anything right. I can't begin to describe how nervous I am about the next conference."
>
> "It's possible nobody will like the food, the speaker won't show up, and I've booked the wrong cars for the VIPs. I'm a walking one-woman disaster."
>
> "All this worrying is making me sick – is it really that important? What's the worst that will happen if everything does go wrong? The delegates will complain and I'll have a warning from my boss. It's not a nice thought, but it's not life-threatening."
>
> "And next week, when it's all over and I'm organizing the next conference, what then? I probably won't even remember feeling like this, and I'm sure no one else will give a thought to my conference. I'm blowing things way out of proportion."

A Positive Attitude

By putting things in context, Marcie realized she was overreacting to things that hadn't yet happened. She also recognized that even if everything went as badly as she imagined, the consequences weren't so bad – she'd feel embarrassed, uncomfortable, and maybe a little ashamed, but that's all.

As Marcie has shown, putting things in context is a very powerful technique that can help you overcome even the most extreme negative thoughts.

The technique of looking for the positive is not only a way of overcoming negative thinking – it's a way of changing your outlook so that you look for the good in situations instead of the bad. In every situation, however bad, things could always be worse, and that's at the heart of looking for the positive.

Maybe the only good thing to draw from problems is that you'll learn from your mistakes, but often you can draw truly positive experiences from them.

If your slides didn't work in your presentation, you'll know to prepare more effectively next time. Was everything really a disaster? Maybe people commented favorably on your speaking voice, your choice of venue, and your knowledge of the product – all positive aspects of a "disastrous" presentation.

Marcie is at her wit's end. She's in the middle of a conference and there seem to be endless problems with the venue. The kitchen hasn't prepared the meals for delegates with special dietary requirements, there aren't enough seats in the conference auditorium, and the main speaker can't be heard at the back of the room. Marcie is determined not to be overcome by negative thoughts.

Marcie 1

"I guess I should have checked with the kitchen to make sure they knew about the special meals. I'd sent a fax, but next time I'll know to speak to the restaurant manager and get confirmation. On the upside, most of the delegates are very pleased with their meals."

Marcie 2

"The feedback about our main speaker was excellent; I'll definitely use her again. It's just unfortunate that she couldn't be heard at the back because there was no microphone. In the future, I'll use a smaller room and limit the number of delegates."

When you challenge your negative thinking, you'll learn valuable lessons from the situations you face, and you'll be able to avoid overreacting to or overdramatizing problems that can be solved.

Whatever technique you use to challenge negative thinking, your focus must be on being realistic and objective in your responses to situations. Each of the four techniques has at its core a recognition that things are rarely as bad as you perceive them to be.

Don't challenge everything your inner voice tells you. Only challenge those things that are having a destructive influence on your state of mind.

If the voice in your head says "You shouldn't have been late," this is a rational and useful comment, not a harmful negative thought.

It isn't always possible to ignore the voice in your head that criticizes you and undermines your confidence.

But that doesn't mean you have to believe what the voice says.

Challenge the voice, and challenge your negative thoughts. You'll find that positive thinking can help you find the best in the situations you face.

33

Reacting Positively to Criticism

Unfortunately, you don't have control over what people say to you – but you do have control over how you respond.

One of the most difficult times to respond to someone is when you are being criticized, particularly when that criticism does not appear to be constructive or even justified.

An inability to accept or handle criticism, even when it's constructive and in your best interest, results in a negative attitude toward both the criticism itself and the critic.

The key to reacting positively to criticism is to take three simple actions:

- agree with the truth of the criticism
- agree with the logic of the critic
- acknowledge that improvement is possible.

If there is truth in the criticism, acknowledge this when dealing with the critic, and don't avoid the issue. When criticism is aimed at something you're uncomfortable talking about, you often dispute even undeniable facts to try to halt the conversation, but this usually has the opposite effect.

Do

Do agree with the truth, and if appropriate, apologize. Saying that the critic is right and that you're sorry is a good way of putting an end to the conversation.

Don't

Don't deny the facts of the situation, even if you feel you've been unfairly treated. Making excuses, arguing about whose fault it is, or trying to shift blame away from yourself will only extend the criticism.

Oliver and Jim are working together on a building project. Oliver has asked to speak to Jim about the fact that the project is behind schedule. Follow along to find out how Jim reacts.

Oliver: I'm concerned that you haven't hit the deadline on the phase 1 deliverables you agreed to.

Jim: That's not true. I've done everything I said I would.

Oliver: Well, you put the schedule together, and you don't seem to know what you're supposed to be doing. You haven't finished the interim report, which was due yesterday.

Jim's negative approach to Oliver's criticism resulted in an escalation of the problem – and more stress for Jim.

Instead of admitting that he'd missed the deadline, Jim became defensive and denied the truth, which simply resulted in Oliver criticizing him further for failing to review the schedule properly.

N ow follow along to find out what happens when Jim agrees with the truth of Oliver's criticism.

Oliver: I'm concerned that you haven't hit the deadline on the phase 1 deliverables you agreed to.

Jim: I know I haven't finished the interim report. I'm sorry. I took on too much and now I'm finding it difficult to meet my commitments.

This time, Jim wasn't negative. He admitted that he'd missed the deadline and immediately defused the situation with Oliver.

A critic's perspective on a situation will be different from yours. As a result, you might feel that a critic is being unfair. You must accept that the critic has a valid view and that his suggestion might work, even if you don't adhere to his thinking.

Agreeing with the logic doesn't mean saying you'll take action.

If your critic proposes a solution that you're reluctant to adopt, simply agree that his suggestion is a good one without committing to take action.

Don't argue with acceptable and reasonable logic, and don't attack the critic – this will lead to an argument.

F ollow along as Jim agrees with the logic of Oliver's suggestion.

Oliver: How about we work on it together to see if we can finish the interim report now? I've got time if you have.

Jim: That's not a bad idea, but I've got a lot of information at my desk. Can I review it and get back to you?

Oliver: Well, let me know how you want to proceed. I'm anxious to get back on track.

When Oliver suggested that they work together on the interim report, Jim agreed that Oliver's suggestion was a good one; in other words, he accepted the logic of what Oliver said. However, even though he accepted Oliver's logic, he did not accept the offer of help.

That way, Jim knew that Oliver would feel like Jim was open to his suggestion but Jim didn't have to commit to doing things Oliver's way. Both parties were pleased with the outcome.

However much you might feel that there's nothing more that can be done, you need to step back and think rationally about what the critic is saying.

It may well be that you can change things to improve the situation – unless things are perfect already.

When your critic suggests that you could do better, respond by saying, "There may be some areas that could improve." This is a good way of acknowledging that improvement is possible while avoiding committing to changes.

It's tempting to claim that you can't do any better, or even to attack the critic's own abilities, but this only escalates bad feelings. If you reverse the criticism by challenging the critic, he'll try to prove you wrong – and the disagreement will escalate.

F ollow along to find out what happens when Jim challenges Oliver's criticism instead of accepting that there may be room for improvement.

Oliver: Have you decided how to proceed? As I said, I'm more than willing to help you create the report if it will help us get back on track. After all, something has to be done.

Jim: I don't need your help, Oliver. I said I'll do it, and I will. I'm doing the best I can.

Oliver: Well, that's easy to say, but we're already behind. We need to find a way of getting back on track, and staying there.

Jim: So, you think you can do better, do you? Fine. Here's my information. You can write the report.

Oliver: At least if I do it myself, I'll know it's going to get done. I was only trying to help. There was no need for you to react so aggressively.

Jim clearly felt threatened by Oliver's criticism and didn't want to accept that there was anything he could do to improve the situation. Instead of graciously declining Oliver's offer of help, Jim became hostile toward Oliver and turned the criticism back on him.

As a result, Oliver criticized Jim for being aggressive. Needless to say, Jim and Oliver's relationship deteriorated.

N ow follow along to find out how different things are when Jim acknowledges that improvement is possible.

A Positive Attitude

Oliver: Have you decided how to proceed? As I said, I'm more than willing to help you create the report if it will help us get back on track. After all, something has to be done.

Jim: I agree. I've taken on too much. That's why I'm behind schedule.

Oliver: So, what's the solution?

Jim: I'll focus on getting the report finished, and then I'll review the schedule. If we can get together later in the day, we can look at the schedule together.

This time, Jim wasn't combative. Although he didn't want help from Oliver, Jim reacted calmly and reasonably to Oliver's request for an update. By admitting that he had taken on too much work, he was acknowledging that there was room for improvement.

Jim could have stopped there, but he went a step further and committed to reviewing the schedule to avoid future problems. Hopefully, this additional step will keep Oliver from voicing future criticism.

Agreeing with the truth and logic of criticism isn't a commitment to behavioral change. Neither is acknowledging that improvement is possible. These three approaches merely limit the potential conflict that could arise from your instinctive need to retaliate.

They help you to avoid feeling bad about yourself, even when the criticism is justified. By agreeing with the critic verbally, you'll avoid negative feelings and be able to react positively to the feedback or criticism that you receive.

Karen was criticizing you because she wanted your performance to improve. By acknowledging the truth of her words, and agreeing with her logic, you should have been able to take her criticism in a positive way. You also had to allow some room for improvement.

If you tried to deny the truth, or retaliated by being aggressive, this would have negatively impacted upon your relationship with Karen.

Remember, you have control over how you react to other's comments. Use that control to your advantage, and let it help you to develop a positive attitude and react positively to the feedback that you receive.

34

Being Assertive

Feeling out of control is one of the most common triggers for negative thinking. If you feel as if you can't influence what happens to you, then you begin to lack confidence and believe the worst is inevitable.

One of the best ways to cope with situations that make you feel negative is to define your boundaries – that means defining what you will or will not tolerate. To do this, you need to be assertive. There are two steps you need to follow:

- Get attention.
- Command a positive response.

When you're asked to do something you don't want to do, it can be tempting to be aggressive or defensive, or to simply concede without discussion.

Being assertive means stating your case in a forceful manner, without being aggressive.

If you feel like you're being taken advantage of, or if you simply don't want to comply with a request, you need to get the attention of the person doing the requesting. Getting attention doesn't mean being rude or unhelpful – that gets you noticed for all of the wrong reasons. It means finding a time when it's appropriate to talk and then calmly explaining your perspective.

Choosing the time

You should deal with issues quickly, but you want to choose a time when you aren't feeling angry or irritated. It's often a good idea to wait until after you've had a "cooling off" period. You should also make sure you can discuss the issue without distractions.

Explaining the facts

You need to explain why you are unhappy or unwilling to comply with a request. Avoid language that is critical or accusatory, and stick to the facts of the situation. It is also helpful to offer a concession to the other person to show that you are being reasonable.

T ed and Michelle work together. Michelle isn't good at organizing her time, and when deadlines approach, she often relies on Ted to help her out. Follow along as Michelle asks Ted for help yet again.

Michelle: Ted, I know you're busy, but I'm in a fix. I haven't finished the programming for the phase 1 prototype, and it has to be finished by Tuesday. You don't mind working the weekend with me to get it finished do you?

Ted: Can we talk about this later Michelle? I'm in the middle of an important piece of work at the moment.

Michelle: Oh, OK. I guess so. Later then.

Ted has been feeling negative about the way his colleagues take advantage of him, and so he is trying a new tactic – being assertive.

Ted

"Michelle always does this, and it isn't fair. I have my own work to do. I was so angry with her today that I had to take some time to calm down."

Michelle

"I can't believe it. Usually Ted is such a soft touch. He's a nice guy and will always help out. We all know that we can rely on 'good old Ted.'"

T ed has decided that he isn't prepared to help Michelle this weekend because he has personal and work commitments of his own. Follow along as Ted catches up with Michelle during a coffee break.

Ted: Michelle, have you got time to talk?

Michelle: Sure, I'm on a break. I guess you want to talk about what you can do to help me with this programming. I don't think it will take all weekend.

Ted: The thing is, Michelle, I have commitments of my own this weekend. I'm behind on one of my own projects, so I need to work on that, and I've also promised to take my son to his Little League game.

Michelle: Oh.

Ted: I know you were hoping I could help out, but I don't have a lot of time. I could try to free up some time tomorrow morning or on Monday if that helps.

Ted did a great job of getting Michelle's attention. He didn't talk to her when he was feeling angry; he waited until he had time to think about her request and calm down.

When he did speak to Michelle, he chose a time when they could speak openly and without distractions. Although Michelle assumed that Ted was going to agree to her request fully, Ted stuck to his strategy and explained the facts.

By telling Michelle why he was unable to help her out, he was reasonable and fair.

He also offered a concession by offering time, during working hours, to support her.

Once you have the attention of the person you're trying to negotiate with, you need to get the response you want – a positive one. It isn't always easy to get the response you're looking for. Being assertive means working on your own behalf to secure an outcome that you're happy with.

Asking For Help

When you've made the other person aware of the facts of your situation, you need to get him to buy-in to helping you. You can do this by inviting him to change the situation or by getting him to see the problem from your perspective. Remain calm and reasonable, even if the response is negative.

Recycling Your Message

Show that you would appreciate a serious offer, possibly to withdraw the request or to compromise. If no offer is forthcoming or if you disagree with the other person's proposal, make a proposal yourself. Being assertive means being forceful and not caving in to pressure at this point.

T ed and Michelle's discussion moves on as Ted tries to command a positive response from Michelle. Follow along to find out what happens.

A Positive Attitude

Michelle: You're telling me you don't have the time to help me? I don't believe this. I rely on you to pitch in and help at the last minute. I don't know what I'm going to do. How can you let me down like this?

Ted: To be fair, Michelle, I think you need to look at this from where I'm standing. I've got my own work to do, and my own commitments.

Michelle: Whatever. So you're saying you can help me tomorrow and on Monday, right?

Ted: That's right. I can help you tomorrow morning or on Monday. I can't do more than that.

Michelle: I'd appreciate your help tomorrow morning if that's OK with you. I'll work the weekend and see what happens on Monday. Thanks, Ted.

Ted did a great job of commanding a positive response. Despite Michelle's initial disbelief, Ted continued to be assertive by getting her to look at things from his perspective.

When Michelle came back to Ted with a proposal – to use the time that Ted had offered – he recycled his message by restating the facts without giving in to Michelle.

At the end of the discussion, Ted had a positive response from Michelle. Instead of agreeing to all of her demands, he responded assertively to Michelle and reached a compromise that both he and Michelle were happy with.

A positive outcome for both sides.

Being assertive can help you halt negative feelings.

To reach a position where you and Adam can share a desk amicably, you need to be assertive. Choosing a time when you can approach the issue in a calm and rational way is the first step to getting Adam's attention and to reaching a resolution.

When you do talk to Adam about the desk, it's important to explain the issue in a factual way with no hint of personal criticism or accusation.

Sometimes, no matter how much you hint at a solution, it is necessary to put forward your own proposal to command a positive response.

This should always be done in a nonaccusatory, and nonjudgmental way if you are to get the outcome you seek.

You are entitled to insist on having your boundaries respected, and assertiveness steps are powerful tools to enable you to do this. Identify situations where it is appropriate and start to use them.

Part V

Lifelong Learning

A lifelong learner knows how to apply existing knowledge and acquire new skills. Lifelong learners are also self-motivated and accept responsibility for identifying and achieving their learning needs.

35

Identifying Learning Needs

"Learning is not attained by chance; it must be sought for with ardor and attended to with diligence." – Abigail Adams, American letter writer and first lady, wife of John Adams

The quote from Abigail Adams is relevant to the need for continuous learning in the 21st-century workplace. Learning has become the basis for employees to stay ahead of the current competitive and ever-changing markets. Employees who continue to acquire new skills on the job will ensure their employability.

Continuing to learn in the workplace requires a proactive attitude, one that is associated with being a lifelong learner. Lifelong learners take charge of their own learning and don't wait to be told what to learn.

A lifelong learner knows how to apply existing knowledge and acquire new skills. Lifelong learners are also self-motivated and accept responsibility for identifying and achieving their learning needs.

Reflect

Think about what motivates you to learn. Perhaps your motivation to learn has to do with getting ahead in your job or gaining financial security. What motivates you to learn?

A learning plan is a written road map for initiating and continuing your career and professional development. There is no single template for creating a learning plan. However, many plans contain the four sections given here.

Career Assessment

The career assessment section offers you the chance to examine your career values, interests, and motivating skills. You will use this information to identify your learning needs.

Career Focus

The career focus section centers around your goals and the learning objectives that will help you achieve them.

Learning Strategy

The learning strategy section is where you will develop the specific strategy for each of your learning objectives. Here, you will note each task required to achieve the learning objective, the learning resources you'll need, and the target completion date.

Means For Evaluation

The means for evaluation section ensures that the tasks that make up your learning strategies are measurable or have verifiable criteria for success. In this section, you will describe the method you'll use to evaluate whether you accomplished your tasks successfully.

The third and final lesson covers a potential learning resource that you might include in the learning strategy section of your learning plan: working with a mentor.

Specifically, this third lesson will teach you what qualities to look for in a mentor and what qualities that you, the protégé, should have to ensure a successful relationship with your mentor.

So you want to climb the corporate ladder, do you? Or maybe you've been thinking about changing careers. Perhaps you've never had a job, or it has been years since you had one.

No matter your circumstances or dreams for the future, one thing is certain: you're going to have to learn new skills and behaviors if you want to move from where you are in life to where you want to be.

But before you jump into learning those new skills and behaviors, it's a good idea to first determine what it is you want, what it is you need, and what it is you have to do to get what you want and need.

Making these determinations will help you identify your learning needs and establish your learning objectives.

Learning Needs

Learning needs are the skills and knowledge that must be acquired for career and professional development to occur.

Learning Objectives

Learning objectives are statements that explain what you will be able to do at the conclusion of instructional activities.

It's important that you identify your learning needs because this process will enhance your self-awareness and make it easier to establish the right learning objectives for you.

Establishing the right learning objectives is important because they will keep you on the path toward your goals.

Take Carrie, for example. After she earned her bachelor's degree in liberal arts, Carrie was offered a job as copywriter in an advertising agency. She had always been creative, so she accepted the position.

But after two years of creative copywriting while on tight deadlines, Carrie was exhausted and dissatisfied; she didn't know what she wanted to do, but she knew that copywriting wasn't it. Right around that time, she met Ben, a career counselor whom she started to work with.

F ollow along as Carrie explains how Ben helped her understand the importance of identifying her learning needs.

"The first thing Ben had me do was identify my learning needs. I did this by writing down my values, my interests, and the skills I like to use. Until I did this exercise, I thought I knew who I was. But I had never really taken the time to sit down and think about it."

"It turns out that even though I'm creative, being able to be creative at work isn't something I am all that interested in. And even though I like writing, it isn't a skill that I want to use all the time."

"Instead, I like to feel that I'm making a difference; I like children and would be very interested in working more with them. And I'd like to use the knowledge I gained about history and my interest in current events on a much more regular basis."

"If I hadn't sat down and really evaluated what was important to me, I wouldn't have known these things about myself. Also, I would have created learning objectives that had nothing to do with how I truly feel. I might have wound up in yet another job I didn't like."

By identifying her learning needs, Carrie became more self-aware. That self-awareness made it easier for her to establish the right learning objectives.

Identifying Learning Needs

"After identifying my learning needs, I realized that what I really wanted to do was teach history and civics."

Developing Learning Objectives

"Ben asked me a lot of questions about my decision to become a teacher. My answers became the learning objectives that would help me reach my goal."

Carrie knew she wanted to be a teacher, but didn't know what grade level she wanted to teach. So one of her first objectives was to identify which grade level appealed to her the most. She also didn't have a teaching certificate; obviously, she was going to need to get one, and that became another objective.

All of Carrie's learning objectives specifically pointed her in the direction she needed to go to reach her goal of becoming a teacher. By planning in advance as Ben suggested, Carrie knew what she wanted to do and how to get there.

The first step toward becoming a lifelong learner is to develop a learning plan. A learning plan is a written road map for initiating and continuing your career and professional development. This lesson covers the first two sections of a learning plan: career assessment and career focus.

Career assessment offers you the chance to examine your career values, interests, and motivating skills. You will use this information to identify your learning needs.

Career focus centers around your goals, the learning objectives that will help you achieve those goals, and the tasks you will have to undertake to accomplish your objectives.

36

Identifying Your Learning Needs

"You've got to be very careful if you don't know where you are going because you might not get there." – Yogi Berra, baseball player and coach

Yogi Berra was gifted at stating the obvious, often with hilarious results. But his comments were also grounded in common sense.

Of course you won't get where you're going if you don't know where you're going. But it's amazing how many people assume that they will achieve their dreams even though they haven't developed a strategy to do so.

The first step toward knowing where you're going – in other words, toward creating a learning plan – is to identify your learning needs. Learning needs are the skills and knowledge that must be acquired for career and professional development to occur.

To identify your learning needs, you can take career assessments and engage in self-discovery activities. Career assessments are made up of questions designed to help you identify your skills and career interests.

Self-discovery activities are assessments you can take and games you can play to learn more about yourself. Many people engage in self-discovery activities that help pinpoint their values and personality traits.

The first section of your learning plan, career assessment, should pertain to your identified learning needs. Specifically, this section should contain information about:

- your career values
- your career interests
- the job skills that motivate you.

Career values are concepts and views that define your professional beliefs and principles. Examples of career values include life-work balance, order and structure, glamour, independence, teamwork, and customer focus.

Life-Work Balance

Seth is a financial analyst who values life-work balance. He is married with three children, and he is a competitive cyclist. He works efficiently to meet client expectations in an average of eight hours a day so that he can attend to his other priorities at the end of his workday.

Order And Structure

Denise is an accounts payable manager who values order and structure. Her profession allows her to follow a predictable schedule and explicitly stated rules. She has a routine for processing, accounting, and financial reporting of accounts payable transactions.

Glamour

Devin enjoys an alluring lifestyle as an international management consultant. He is responsible for high-profile accounts. He travels to Paris, London, Amsterdam, Tokyo, and Hong Kong to analyze and propose ways to improve organizational structure, efficiency, and profits.

Independence

Nancy is a journalist who values independence. She likes to determine the nature of her work without significant direction from others. She selects the focus and content of her newspaper articles with limited input from others.

Teamwork

Michelle is part of a web design team that works closely to create winning web solutions. The team collaborates to assess customer needs, create web designs, and address customer issues. It uses collaborative software to share files, data, and projects.

Customer Focus

Harry is a technical support engineer who values customer focus. He places the interests of clients ahead of personal or organizational interests. Harry seeks feedback from clients and incorporates the feedback to improve quality, productivity, and customer service.

Paul is a senior technical support engineer who is responsible for providing quality technical support to internal and external customers. This involves supporting, analyzing, and testing his company's software.

Paul provides team members with assistance in resolving customer issues and completing support projects. He enjoys the challenge of applying his knowledge to problems presented by customers.

Paul feels job satisfaction when customers and colleagues express their gratitude for his assistance.

Which career values pertain to Paul?

The career values that pertain to Paul are appreciation, problem solving, and mental challenge.

Appreciation

Paul values being acknowledged in private for his efforts. When customers express their gratitude for his assistance, he feels a sense of job satisfaction.

Problem Solving

Paul values problem solving, or working to remove obstacles and finding solutions to difficult problems. He helps customers find solutions to their problems.

Mental Challenges

Paul values the mental challenge presented by his work. He is involved in activities that allow him to exercise his knowledge of his company's software.

The career assessment section also includes career interests. Career interests are professional fields that are best suited for you based on your preferences. These interests can be placed into six categories: hands-on, scientific, artistic, social, enterprising, and conventional.

Hands-On

People who prefer to work with animals, tools, or machines are interested in hands-on careers. They are skilled with tools, mechanical or electrical drawings, machines, plants, or animals.

Scientific

People who prefer solving math and science problems are interested in scientific careers. They typically avoid leading, selling, or persuading activities. Those interested in scientific careers see themselves as precise, methodical, and intellectual.

Artistic

People who gravitate toward creative activities such as visual art, dance, music, or writing are interested in artistic careers. They generally avoid highly ordered or repetitive activities. They see themselves as expressive, original, and independent.

Social

People who like to engage in activities that help people, such as teaching, nursing, giving first aid, or informing, have an interest in social careers. They avoid using machines or tools to achieve goals. They see themselves as helpful, friendly, and trustworthy.

Enterprising

People who enjoy leading and persuading others, as well as selling products and ideas, have an interest in enterprising careers. They avoid activities that require careful observation and analytical thinking. They perceive themselves as energetic, ambitious, and sociable.

Conventional

People who prefer to work with numbers, records, or machines in an orderly way are interested in conventional careers. They avoid ambiguous, unstructured activities. They perceive themselves as orderly and good at following a set plan.

After you have determined your career interests, the next step is to identify the occupations that fall within your category of interest.

Hands-On

Examples of hands-on occupations include mechanical engineer, ultrasound technologist, carpenter, microelectronics technician, firefighter, and geologist.

Scientific

Examples of scientific occupations include surgeon, botanist, anthropologist, psychiatrist, software engineer, and market research analyst.

Artistic

Examples of artistic occupations include architect, screenwriter, fashion designer, choreographer, sculptor, photojournalist, music teacher, and cartoonist.

Social

Examples of social occupations include nurse-midwife, coach, teacher, social worker, employee relations specialist, minister, loan officer, and physical therapist.

Enterprising

Examples of enterprising occupations include communications consultant, patent agent, art director, tax attorney, motion pictures producer, industrial-health engineer, and advertising sales representative.

Conventional

Examples of conventional occupations include credit analyst, medical record technician, accountant, and computer operator.

Most people will feel an affinity toward several of the six categories of career interests. And many of the combinations are complementary.

For example, if you prefer to work with animals and you enjoy science and math, your interests lie within the hands-on and scientific categories. These two categories can be combined to provide a variety of occupations that may appeal to you, such as veterinarian, marine biologist, or wildlife conservationist.

Learning about your career interests can also help you identify occupations that probably won't fulfill your needs.

For example, if your interests lie within the social and artistic categories, becoming a surgeon is probably not an ideal occupation for you.

Remember Paul, the senior technical support engineer responsible for providing quality technical support to internal and external customers? He assists team members in resolving customer issues and completing support projects and enjoys the challenge of solving technical problems encountered by customers.

Think about what his top two categories of career interests and his preferred occupations might be.

Paul's Career Interests

Paul's top two categories of career interests are scientific and social. He enjoys solving problems related to his company's software, and he gets satisfaction from helping his customers.

Paul's Preferred Occupations

Paul's preferred occupations are software trainer and computer support specialist. Trainers instruct learners in the use of software applications. Support specialists interpret problems and provide technical support for hardware, software, and systems.

Assessing your own career interests helps you zero in on appropriate occupations. Without such an assessment, it is very difficult to select an occupation when you have thousands to choose from.

Job skills that motivate you are also important to include in the career assessment section. Job skills make up the expertise needed to effectively perform a given job. Examples of job skills include planning meeting agendas, selling products, negotiating deals, and defining performance standards.

To create your list of job skills, you can include the skills you have acquired in former occupations and positions with other companies and volunteer work. Also include the skills you want to improve, and the skills you're interested in attaining.

Next, determine which skills you are interested in using. After you've written down all these job skills, decide which ones interest you the most.

Do this by ranking the job skills in order of preference. You may have already narrowed the list of occupations you're interested in, so your ranking should include the skills required for your chosen occupation. These skills should be ranked high; if not, you should consider pursuing another occupation.

Paul, the technical support engineer, gets the most job fulfillment from interfacing with customers. He also delights in resolving technical issues. Paul gets satisfaction from supporting team members with their support incidents.

Because Paul is in his element when helping others solve technical problems, he is less interested in working alone to analyze and test software. Nonetheless, he enjoys it in short stretches.

Completing the career assessment section of a learning plan allowed you to discover your career values, your career interests, and the job skills that motivate you. This information revealed that software sales is a better fit for you.

Had you not completed the career assessment section, you would not have identified a more satisfying professional direction than computer programming.

Learning more about your career values, your career interests, and the job skills that appeal to you will help you identify your learning needs. And that's the first step toward knowing where you're going.

37

Establishing Your Learning

Objectives

How would you define the word "objective"?

A goal is the end to which you direct your efforts.

Objectives are often used to help people reach their goals. For the lifelong learner, an objective is often known as a learning objective. Learning objectives are statements that explain exactly what the learner will be able to do at the conclusion of instructional activities.

Lifelong learners apply learning objectives to their learning plan after they have identified the specific skills, knowledge, and abilities they want to acquire or enhance.

These learning objectives become the building blocks for reaching their goals.

The second section of a learning plan – career focus – centers around your goals and the learning objectives that will help you achieve them. An effective learning objective should:

- pertain to its corresponding goal
- explain what skill, knowledge, or ability you will have upon its completion.

As you just learned, an effective learning objective should pertain to its corresponding goal. It should be

---

Channeling Your Inner Boss   211 framed in such a way that it's a required step in reaching a goal.

Effective Objective

An effective learning objective for becoming a project manager is, "I will create project schedules and budgets using project management software."

Ineffective Objective

An ineffective learning objective for becoming a project manager is, "I will be able to use web design software to create web pages."

An effective learning objective also explains what skill, knowledge, or ability you will have upon its completion. The objective must be more specific than vague, and more narrow than broad. But, it can't be too specific, because that will take it down to task level. A task is a concrete, measurable event.

Effective Objective

An effective learning objective for becoming a project manager is, "I will receive certification in project management." This objective states what you will have when you complete your educational pursuits.

Ineffective Objective

An ineffective learning objective for becoming a project manager is, "I will learn all I can about managing projects." This objective is too broad and does not state what you will be able to do when you complete your educational pursuits.

Charlotte is a business analyst with a consulting firm. Her goal is to become a senior associate in nine months. One of the jobs of a senior associate is to make weekly presentations to clients; another is to lead a team.

Which are the most effective learning objectives:

I will organize and deliver professional client presentations.

This objective is effective because it pertains to Charlotte's goal and explains what skills she will have upon its completion. In order to become a senior associate, Charlotte must be a skilled presenter.

I will improve my presentation skills

Although this objective pertains to Charlotte's goal, it does not explain exactly what skill, knowledge, or ability Charlotte will have upon its completion.

I will effectively facilitate team meetings.

This objective is effective because it pertains to Charlotte's goal and explains what skills she will have upon its completion. To become a senior associate,

Charlotte must be able to effectively facilitate team meetings.

I will work with my mentor to develop skills in research techniques
This objective is ineffective because it does not explain what skill, knowledge, or ability Charlotte will have upon its completion. The objective also does not pertain to Charlotte's goal of becoming a senior associate. She does not need research skills as a senior associate.

I will go the extra mile in demonstrating my initiative at work
This objective is ineffective because it is too broad, and doesn't pertain to Charlotte's goal. The objective doesn't explain exactly what skill, knowledge, or ability Charlotte will have upon its completion.

When constructed correctly, your learning objectives will help you achieve your learning goals.

38

Learning Strategies for Evaluation

Imagine you've identified your learning needs, determined your learning goals, and constructed the appropriate learning objectives. All you need to do now is achieve those objectives, right?

In fact, you need to develop a learning strategy and a way to evaluate the learning objectives you've set.

The last two sections of your learning plan will allow you to do just that.

A learning plan is a written road map for initiating and continuing career and professional development. The last two sections of a learning plan are named learning strategy and means for evaluation.

These last two sections are very important because they will:

- focus your efforts
- ensure your accountability.

Jack, a copywriter in an advertising agency, was ready for a career change. After completing the career assessment and career focus sections of his learning plan, he knew that he wanted to be a teacher.

Jack's learning strategies and means for evaluation allowed him to focus his efforts. He listed each task, its resources, and its completion date.

His means for evaluation ensured his accountability. Jack wrote down the questions he was accountable for in regard to each task. His criteria were mainly, "Was it done?" and, "Was it done on time?"

To achieve your learning objectives, it's critical that you complete the road map known as your learning plan. Formulating a learning strategy and means for evaluation for each objective will focus your efforts and ensure your accountability.

39

Formulating a Learning Strategy

How will you go about attaining new skills or improving existing ones to achieve your professional dreams?

Successful lifelong learners know that after developing their learning objectives, they should develop a learning strategy for each objective.

The three steps for completing the learning strategy section of a learning plan are:

1. listing the tasks that compose each objective
2. identifying the learning resources required for each task
3. choosing a realistic target completion date for each task.

The first step is to list the tasks that compose each objective. A task is an action that must occur if objectives are to be achieved. To be effective, a task should be concrete and specific. Describe how you plan to carry out the task and what process you plan to follow to accomplish your objective. When tasks must be performed in succession, list them sequentially.

For example, tasks could include reading and studying, conducting interviews, performing experiments, taking a course, and researching.

A task may be something specific like writing a report, or it may be something general like getting information. If your task seems too broad, describe it in such a way that it becomes specific.

For example, instead of writing, "I will get information about degree programs," break it up to form two specific actions.

Task 1

I will generate a list of questions about degree programs.

Task 2

I will visit the web sites of the three colleges in my area to discover the answers to my questions.

The second step is to identify the learning resources required for each task. Learning resources are the people you plan to consult and the tools you plan to use to help you acquire the desired skill, knowledge, or ability.

You can find learning resources internally, within your organization, and externally. Some examples of internal learning resources are in-house training workshops and company-sponsored seminars, online training courses, and certification programs.

Additional examples include mentors, coworkers, vendors, and suppliers. You can also learn from challenging projects for which you can volunteer, such as laboratory trials and field experience.

External learning resources include formal academic courses and programs; teachers and instructors; professional association involvement, including conferences, monthly meetings, and networking events with other professionals in your field; books; manuals; and a variety of learning technologies, including computers and the Internet.

The third step is to choose a realistic target completion date for each task. Realistic means that you allow yourself enough time to perform your regular job duties when setting a target completion date. However, you should not set the date so far in the future that you forget about it.

Realistic also means that you don't set a date that's at the same time as a work deadline. Some target completion dates will already be set for you by external factors, such as application deadlines and conference dates.

Linda, the employee relations specialist, is involved in a demanding employee relations project that begins today, January 15, with a deadline of March 1. She and her team members expect to work ten-hour days for six weeks prior to the deadline.

Despite this project, she wants to move forward with her learning strategy. Linda plans to start working on her learning strategy on February 1.

Task 1

"I will create a list of questions to ask when
I contact mediation programs."

February 3

A target completion date of February 3 for creating a list of questions for mediation programs is unrealistic. Because Linda is involved in a demanding employee relations project, she must give herself more time for such a task.

February 20

A target completion date of February 20 is realistic because it gives Linda enough time to complete the task, especially given her demanding workload. It is also not so far ahead that she will forget about the task.

Task 2

> "I will contact mediators to generate recommendations for mediation certification programs."

March 10

A target completion date of March 10 is realistic. It gives Linda enough time to complete the task, given her deadline on March 1. This date is not so far ahead that she will forget about the task.

April 15

A target completion date of April 15 is too far ahead for this task. If Linda were to establish this date as the target completion date, she would run the risk of forgetting about the task.

Task 3

"I will create a list of recommended mediation certification programs in my area."

March 1

A target completion date of March 1 is unrealistic; this task must be performed after Linda contacts mediators. Also, this is the same date as the employee relations project deadline, an important deadline for Linda's work.

March 15

A target completion date of March 15 is realistic; it gives Linda enough time to complete both the task and her project responsibilities.

The three steps for completing the learning strategy section of a learning plan are to sequentially list the tasks that compose each objective, to identify the learning resources required for each task, and to choose a realistic target completion date for each task.

If one of the three steps is inconclusive or missing altogether, the learning strategy will not be effective in helping you meet your learning objective.

It's important that you address all three steps for completing an effective learning strategy. The three steps are:

1. listing the tasks that compose each objective
2. identifying the learning resources required for each task

3. choosing a realistic target completion date for each task.

To determine what tasks you must perform to carry out your objective, identify the measurable events that must occur if the objective is to be achieved. Create a flowchart or a list in which you write the required tasks.

If one task relies on another, then list those tasks sequentially. If tasks are sequential, document the step-by-step instructions for performing the process. Ask yourself, "What should I do first, second, third, and so on?"

Colleen is a project manager whose goal is to attain project management professional (PMP) certification. In talking to a senior project manager at work, she learned about the process she should follow to attain PMP certification.

The senior project manager recommended that Colleen take a PMP certification exam preparation course and use the strategies taught and materials distributed in the course to prepare for the exam.

One of Colleen's objectives is to satisfy the Project Management Institute's Continuing Certification Requirements Program. Her other objective is to pass the PMP examination, scheduled for May 25. She is constructing a learning strategy for the latter learning objective. Colleen will be busy at work until April 30. Her first step is to sequentially list the tasks that compose this objective.

Task 1: Course Selection

"I will select and register for a web-based self-study PMP certification exam preparation course."

Task 2: Course Completion

"I will complete a web-based self-study PMP certification exam preparation course."

Task 3: Exam Preparation

"I will prepare for the PMP certification exam."

Task 4: Exam Completion

"I will take the PMP certification exam."

Next, to complete the second step of formulating a learning strategy, you have to consider the tasks one at a time.

For each task, ask yourself, "What resources do I need to help me carry out this task?" Determine whether you must consult an institution, an expert, a professional organization, a written document, or a web resource.

Colleen consulted a senior project manager at work to identify the required learning resources. She has completed the second step by identifying the learning resources required for each of the tasks that compose her learning objective.

Task 1: course selection

"In order to select a PMP certification exam preparation course, I will contact my local Project Management Institute chapter, post the question to project management mailing lists on the Internet, and visit various project management web sites."

Task 2: course completion

"I will use my laptop and the course provider's web site to take the self-study PMP certification exam preparation course."

Task 3: exam preparation

"To prepare for the PMP certification exam, I will study the Project Management Institute's book, 'A Guide to the Project Management Body of Knowledge' and course materials."

Task 4: exam completion

"I will take the PMP certification exam at a local testing center."

To perform the third step, ask yourself, "What is a realistic target completion date for each task?" Set a realistic target completion date for each task by considering your work demands and pertinent deadlines.

Determine the exact or approximate time required to complete the task. Don't set a date on the same day as a due date you have at work.

Colleen's PMP examination is scheduled for May 25. She will be busy at work until April 30. She has set realistic target completion dates for each of her tasks.

Course selection

"I will select and register for a web-based self-study PMP certification exam preparation course."

May 1
"My target completion date for selecting a PMP exam preparation course is May 1. Although I will be very busy until April 30, a month is enough time to conduct research on various PMP preparation courses."

Course completion

"I will complete a web-based self-study PMP certification exam preparation course."

May 11

"A web-based self-study PMP certification exam preparation course will take 20 hours to complete. I would like to complete the course two weeks before the test. I will start the course on May 3 and finish by May 11."

Exam preparation

"I will prepare for the PMP certification exam."

May 24

"I will complete my PMP certification exam preparation on May 24, the day before the exam on May 25."

Exam completion

"I will take the PMP certification exam."

May 25

"I will take the PMP certification exam on May 25."

One of Colleen's objectives was to pass the PMP certification examination. Her planning process was shaped by the fact that she had registered to take the exam on May 25. Three of the tasks relied on another task, so Colleen listed those tasks sequentially. Colleen also had to factor in her work demands.

Had Colleen not mapped out her learning strategy in this way, she may have overcommitted herself and not allotted enough time for exam preparation. She could have failed the exam and have been required to repeat the process.

You developed a learning strategy for the objective to put together a sales presentation for your interview. You did this by completing the learning strategy section of a learning plan.

First you sequentially listed the tasks that compose each objective. Then you identified the learning resources required for the tasks.

Finally you chose a realistic target completion date for one of the tasks.

By following the three steps, you were able to find your way for achieving your goal of becoming a solution specialist.

Take the time to complete the learning strategy section of your learning plan. It is the most detailed part of the road map you develop for achieving your professional dreams.

40

Developing the Criteria for Evaluation

No learning strategy is complete if it doesn't include a way for you to verify whether you have accomplished each task.

In many learning plans, this information is contained in the fourth section: means for evaluation.

A learning plan is a written road map for initiating and continuing career and professional development.

In the means for evaluation section, you will describe the method you'll use to determine whether you have accomplished your tasks successfully.

The strategies for correctly completing the means for evaluation section of a learning plan are:

- reporting your progress to another stakeholder
- verifying whether you completed the task
- verifying that you met the target date for completion.

One strategy for correctly completing the means for evaluation section is to report your progress to another stakeholder who will be affected by your decision to become a lifelong learner.

A stakeholder could be a supervisor, a mentor, a coworker, a life coach, a career counselor, a team leader, your spouse, or a family member.

If one of your learning goals pertains to the company you're already working for, talk with your supervisor about your learning plan.

Review

Go over your plan in detail with your supervisor. Ask her to help you remain accountable for accomplishing your tasks.

Report

For example, ask her whether she would meet with you the day after each deadline for a task so you can report on its status and ask her any questions you may have.

If your goal is to change careers, then in most cases it's probably inappropriate to consider your current supervisor as a stakeholder. It could be appropriate, though, if you have a close relationship with your supervisor.

Another strategy for establishing means for evaluation is to verify whether you completed the task. If your task is measurable, your criteria must measure the outcome.

Measurable means that the task has verifiable criteria for its success. For example, if your task is to receive 90 percent or higher on an exam, your exam score will be your measurable evaluation criterion.

You can also verify completion of tasks with items that signify completion, such as a certificate from a completed course or training session.

Your evaluation criteria must support your learning objective. For example, imagine you are deciding on a field of medicine to pursue. Your learning objective is to select a specialty, and one of your associated tasks is to conduct interviews with doctors in different specialty areas.

Completed Six Interviews With Doctors

This evaluation criterion is not appropriate because it does not support your learning objective: to select a specialty.

Completed Interviews With Doctors In Six Different Specialty Areas Of Medicine

This evaluation criterion is appropriate. Because you are deciding which area of medicine to pursue, it's imperative that you interview doctors who specialize in different areas.

The last strategy is to verify that you met the target date for completion. If you complete your task by the target date you established for the task, you have met this criterion.

For example, if your goal is to become a published author, and your objective is to submit a magazine article for publication, then one of your tasks might be to complete an article for submission by August 9.

In this case, August 9 would be your target date for completion. By August 10, you would have to verify whether you completed this task.

Colleen, a project manager with a telecommunications company, recently attained her project management professional (PMP) certification. Her goal is to become a senior project manager at a software company. One of her objectives is to land five interviews. Colleen has a formal relationship with her boss.

Task 1

"I'll create a resume and cover letter that highlight my PMP certification and detail my project management experience. I'll start developing my resume and cover letter on May 1."

Observation (Task 1)

Colleen's task does not contain evaluation criteria. She doesn't have a plan to report her progress on resume and cover letter development to another stakeholder, nor does she have a plan for verifying the task. Colleen is also missing a target date for completion.

Task 2

"I'll ask my boss to help me stay accountable for contacting ten potential employers each week by Thursday afternoon. I'll ask her to meet with me on Friday so that I can give her a status report."

Observation (Task 2)

Colleen's task contains inappropriate evaluation criteria. Her boss is not an appropriate stakeholder for this objective. An appropriate choice would be a career counselor or mentor.

The errors displayed by Colleen on the previous page could adversely affect her ability to measure her success.

This will ultimately affect her ability to achieve her learning objective, to schedule interviews, and her learning goal to get a new position as a senior project manager.

As you complete your learning tasks, remember to evaluate their outcomes. Doing so will ensure you're on the right track to achieving your learning objectives, and ultimately, attaining your learning goals.

41

Mentoring

Take a minute to think back over your life. Does anyone stand out as being particularly helpful or insightful? Did anyone ever challenge you – in a way that bolstered your self-esteem – to work harder and become more proficient at something?

Some people remember one or two teachers, coaches, troop leaders, religious leaders, or college advisors who made a difference in their lives.

If you remember someone like this, that person was most likely your mentor, even if neither of you thought of him in those terms.

A mentor has a lot of experience and influence in a chosen field, and he uses it to help and guide another person's – the protégé's – professional development.

A mentor can, but does not have to, work for the same organization that employs the protégé.

Working with a mentor can be a valuable experience for you, no matter how old you are or what stage you're at in your career.

A mentor guides you as you develop and carry out your professional learning plan

Your mentor should ask you questions and help you work through the answers so that you develop the right learning goals, learning objectives, and learning tasks to help you advance in your career and grow professionally.

A mentor can help you become adept as a lifelong learner

After months of working with your mentor, you may begin to strive to learn more and become better on your own. This result could very well continue even after the official relationship with your mentor has ended.

A mentor allows you to examine your performance in a safe environment.

A mentor should offer you her objective opinions regarding your job performance. Because she is your champion and she wants you to succeed, you can listen to and follow up on her advice without feeling threatened.

42

Qualities of an Effective Mentor

Imagine that you and several others have been shipwrecked on an island. Only one person in your group can speak the same language as the locals.

Reflect

In essence, this one person is in charge of your fate. His personal qualities – the ones that reflect his values – will show through his attempts to communicate with the locals. If the locals perceive him in a negative way, they won't help any of you get off the island. What qualities would you hope that this one person has?

Like the island spokesperson, a mentor is a compassionate person who influences your fate. A mentor is someone with a great deal of experience and influence in a chosen field who helps and guides your – the protégé's – professional or career development.

A mentor can, but does not have to, work for the same organization that employs you.

An effective mentor possesses many qualities that allow him to help you develop professionally. If a mentor works for the same firm as you do, he should possess company-specific knowledge. An effective mentor is also:

- experienced
- dedicated
- influential
- credible
- insistent
- verbally adept
- good at listening
- objective
- encouraging.

Company-Specific Knowledge

If a mentor works for the same organization as you, he should know how the organization functions, such as how to get things done and how to advance through the ranks. To be effective, your mentor must also be willing to share his company-specific knowledge.

Experienced

An effective mentor is experienced and is willing to share his skills and expertise. Your mentor's skills and expertise should match your professional development needs and career goals.

Dedicated

A mentor helps you achieve your learning goals. He should participate fully in the mentoring relationship. To show dedication, he must set clear expectations, define roles, determine meeting logistics, and decide how to deal with problems when they arise.

Influential

A mentor should know people throughout the industry – and if applicable, throughout the organization – and be able to introduce you to the ones who can help you reach your learning goals.

Credible

A mentor should be credible within the profession, and if applicable, the organization. His colleagues should respect him, his work, and his opinions.

C harlotte is a business analyst with a consulting firm. Her goal is to become a senior associate within nine months. One of the jobs of a senior associate is to make weekly presentations to clients; another is to lead a team.

Charlotte would like to make progress on her objective to work with a mentor to develop team leadership skills. She has asked Sam, a senior analyst, to be her mentor, and Sam has agreed to take on the role.

Follow along in a conversation where Sam is ineffective in mentoring Charlotte. In other words, Sam does not demonstrate the first five desired qualities here.

Charlotte: Do you have some ideas for working toward a senior associate position? Having been a senior associate yourself, and now a senior analyst, you have the skills and expertise I'm seeking. Can you give me insight into the organizational politics of our firm?

Sam: I know how things work around here, but after all these years, I like to keep a low profile and stay out of organizational politics. My advice to you is to take the path of least resistance.

Charlotte: I see. Well, I'm sure you have some valuable expertise to share with me. So, when and where would you like to meet, and what should our roles be?

Sam: I prefer an informal approach to mentoring. We can leave it open ended and meet whenever a need arises. I'll let you take the lead.

Charlotte: OK. Do you think you can help me connect with the senior partners who make the promotion decisions?

Sam: Perhaps. I'll see what I can do, but I think it's best for you to approach them yourself. That will demonstrate your proactive working style and make the best impression.

Charlotte: Do you have ideas for approaching some of the senior partners? Or can you set something up for me?

Sam: I'm not sure. Ever since we lost the RPJ account, I've felt that my relationship with some of the senior partners has become strained. But I'll see what I can do.

Sam did not display the qualities of an effective mentor in his interaction with Charlotte. As a result, it's likely that she felt frustrated and uncertain about the benefits she would receive from her mentoring relationship with Sam.

Company-Specific Knowledge

Although Sam possessed company-specific knowledge, he did not share it with Charlotte. Instead, he advised her to keep a low profile and stay out of organizational politics. Thus, his knowledge had no real value for Charlotte.

Experience

Sam's expertise matches Charlotte's professional development needs and career goals, but he was not necessarily willing to share his expertise with her. Instead, he advised her to keep a low profile.

Dedication

Sam failed to show dedication by not setting clear expectations with Charlotte. Instead, he told her that he preferred an informal approach. It's unlikely that Sam intends to prioritize his mentoring duties.

Influence

Sam appeared unwilling or unable to use his influence to help Charlotte reach her learning goals. He encouraged her to approach the senior partners herself.

Credibility

Sam's credibility appeared to be in question. He referred to strained relations between himself and some of the senior partners.

F ollow along in a conversation where Sam demonstrates the first five qualities of an effective mentor with Charlotte.

Charlotte: Do you have some ideas for working toward a senior associate position? Having been a senior associate yourself, and now a senior analyst, you have the skills and expertise I'm seeking. Can you give me insight into the organizational politics of our firm?

Sam: Definitely. I can use my influence to help you position yourself as a strong candidate for the senior associate position. It's important to attend the networking events and take the lead on projects. That way, you're visible to the people who make the promotion decisions. I'll make sure you meet all the right people.

Sam: You should know that all of the business analysts I've recommended for senior associate positions have received promotions. I guess my opinion counts for something around here.

Charlotte: I'm sure it does, Sam. So, when and where would you like to meet, and how should we define our mentoring roles?

Sam: Let's meet in my office once a week on Fridays, at 3:00, to create a plan for working toward a senior associate position. That way we can assess your progress every week. Does that sound good?

Charlotte: It sounds perfect, Sam.

In the example on the previous page, Sam demonstrated the qualities of an effective mentor, which encouraged and motivated Charlotte.

Company-Specific Knowledge

Sam shared his company-specific knowledge with Charlotte when he stressed the importance of attending networking events and taking the lead on projects. This information will help Charlotte as she works toward her goal of becoming a senior associate.

Experienced

Sam's skills and expertise match Charlotte's professional development needs and career goals. He worked as a senior associate prior to becoming a senior analyst. His expertise and insights about his own career path will be invaluable to Charlotte.

Dedicated

Sam demonstrated his dedication when he established parameters for his mentoring relationship with Charlotte. He set up a regular meeting time and proposed a plan of action.

Influential

Sam demonstrated his pull when he told Charlotte he would use his influence to help her position herself for the job of senior associate. Sam promised Charlotte that he would introduce her to contacts who could potentially help her achieve her goal.

Credible

When Sam told Charlotte that all the business analysts he had recommended for senior associate positions had been promoted, he demonstrated his credibility. Clearly, his colleagues value his opinions on promotion decisions.

Insistent

A mentor should challenge you to reach beyond what is familiar and comfortable so you can grow from new experiences.

Encouraging

A mentor should provide you with positive encouragement so that you'll be more willing to push yourself beyond your normal boundaries and work through the low spots in your efforts. Additionally, he should encourage you to expand upon your strengths.

Objective

Your mentor is your champion; he wants you to succeed. To effectively assess your strengths and weaknesses, he needs to remain objective and not let feelings or prejudices get in the way. It's OK for your mentor to acknowledge your weaknesses, but he should not let bias be a factor.

Verbally Adept

A mentor should be able to communicate well verbally. His answers and feedback should be clear and concise, and he should be able to give you succinct, pertinent instructions and examples.

Good At Listening

A mentor should listen to what you are telling him about your needs and concerns. That way, the guidance he offers will be relevant to you.

C harlotte and Sam are discussing her objectives. Follow along in a conversation where Sam

---

doesn't demonstrate the remaining five desired qualities.

Charlotte: In order to become a senior associate, I must develop my presentation skills. The only problem is that I have anxiety about speaking in front of groups.

Sam: Yeah, most women have that problem. Perhaps it's best that you avoid that task. It won't reflect well on our company if your client presentations don't go smoothly. If you're uncomfortable with the task of presenting to clients, you can ask another analyst to be the lead presenter.

Charlotte: Good idea. I prefer to let someone who is more skilled handle the client presentations. Thanks for your input. I know I should also become skilled at leading meetings. What should I know about facilitating team meetings?

Sam: Basically, it's important to plan for meetings. Then when you're facilitating meetings, you must pick up on group dynamics and lead the meeting accordingly.

Charlotte: I'm not clear how to approach these tasks. Can you give me some pointers?

Sam: You must observe the interpersonal interactions and intervene when necessary.

Charlotte: I guess I don't understand the point you're trying to make.

Sam: Don't worry, Charlotte, you'll be fine. Now, let's finish this client analysis.

Because Sam did not demonstrate the qualities of an effective mentor during their interaction, Charlotte most likely felt self-doubt and confusion.

Insistent

Sam did not challenge Charlotte to reach beyond her comfort level and grow from new experiences. He encouraged her to avoid public speaking, a task that makes her uncomfortable.

Encouraging

Sam did not encourage Charlotte to push herself beyond her normal boundaries and work through the low spots in her efforts. In fact, he confirmed her fear that she lacked public speaking skills.

Objective

Sam did not stay objective when mentoring Charlotte. He introduced personal bias when assessing her public speaking skills.

Verbally Adept

Sam's answers, feedback, and instructions were vague and imprecise. Charlotte was unclear about his instructions for leading meetings.

A Good Listener

Sam didn't pick up on the need to explain strategies for leading team meetings. He didn't listen to what Charlotte was telling him about her needs and concerns. Instead, he was anxious to finish his task at hand.

F ollow along in a conversation where Sam effectively mentors Charlotte as they discuss her objectives. Sam demonstrates the remaining five qualities.

Charlotte: In order to become a senior associate, I must develop my presentation skills. The only problem is, I have anxiety about speaking in front of groups.

Sam: Anxiety about public speaking is easy to overcome. It just takes practice. You have the poise, presence, and professionalism to be an excellent public speaker, Charlotte. Don't be too hard on yourself if you feel anxiety before your presentation. That's normal.

Charlotte: Thanks for your support. I suppose with practice, I'll learn to overcome the anxiety. I know I should also become skilled at leading meetings. What should I know about facilitating team meetings?

Sam: Leading team meetings requires an agenda, effective time management, strategies for encouraging participation, and a plan for follow up. You must also determine whether it is a decision-making, informational, or problem-solving meeting. I can help you develop these skills.

Charlotte: It sounds as though there's a lot to consider. How do you make sure you perform all the necessary activities?

Sam: You seem tentative about the task. Don't worry – I've noticed that you're a gifted communicator. As we work together, we'll develop a plan to foster your meeting facilitation skills.

Charlotte: Great. I know I'm in good hands.

This time, Sam demonstrated the qualities of an effective mentor, which encouraged and motivated Charlotte and instilled confidence in her.

Insistent

Sam challenged Charlotte to reach beyond what is comfortable and to grow from new experiences. He demonstrated insistence when he told Charlotte that through practice, she could overcome her anxiety with public speaking.

Encouraging

Sam encouraged Charlotte when he told her that she has the poise, presence, and professionalism to be an excellent public speaker. He encouraged Charlotte to push herself beyond her normal boundaries and to work through the low spots in her efforts.

Objective

Sam demonstrated objectivity when he championed Charlotte without showing any preconceived notions about her public speaking skills. He also subtly acknowledged her anxiety without judging her.

Verbally Adept

Sam was verbally adept in his interaction with Charlotte. He provided feedback and answers that were clear and concise. When he explained meeting facilitation, he gave Charlotte succinct, pertinent instructions.

A Good Listener

Sam demonstrated his listening skills when he said he noticed that Charlotte was tentative about the task of meeting facilitation. He listened to Charlotte's concerns and offered relevant guidance.

By demonstrating many of the qualities of an effective mentor, Sharon encouraged Dale to stretch himself professionally. Her listening skills enabled her to offer relevant guidance. Sharon's experience, influence, credibility, and company-specific knowledge will help Dale reach his professional goals.

If Sharon had failed to demonstrate the qualities of an effective mentor, it is likely that Dale would feel self-doubt, confusion, and frustration. He might also question the benefits to be gained from his mentoring relationship with Sharon.

It's difficult to chart the best course for your professional development and learning needs. A mentor can reduce some of that difficulty and offer you valuable guidance.

43

Qualities of an Effective Protégé

Have you ever been in a relationship where you feel as though the other person is always calling the shots? If so, how did that make you feel? Did you ever do anything that you wanted to do?

Mentoring offers you the opportunity to accept guidance and input from an expert in your field; it should not entail handing over complete control of your professional life.

Entering into a mentoring relationship is just like entering into any other type of relationship: both parties have to work to ensure that the relationship results in a win-win situation. An effective protégé is:

- dedicated
- adaptable

- persistent
- responsible.

A protégé should take the time and expend the effort necessary to achieve his learning goals. He should be an active participant in the mentoring relationship; after all, it's his professional development at stake.

Dedicated

To be dedicated, a protégé should take time to achieve his learning goals. Showing dedication includes setting clear expectations with the mentor, defining roles, determining meeting logistics, and deciding how to deal with problems when they arise.

Adaptable

A mentor is a busy professional who is donating valuable time to the protégé. To be adaptable, the protégé should be willing to reschedule appointments and accept that meetings may be interrupted occasionally.

Responsible

A responsible protégé prepares for a meeting with his mentor. Before the meeting, he should provide a list of carefully considered and professional questions to maximize the use of the mentor's time. If that's not possible, he should bring the list to the meeting.

Persistent

Because a mentor is a professional with many demands, she may tend to put other priorities ahead of the protégé more often than she should. The protégé should be persistent in asking for the amount of time he needs to spend with the mentor.

To show dedication, you should establish clear expectations with your mentor by defining the roles and logistics of your mentoring relationship. Without taking the time to establish parameters and ground rules, you may not achieve the learning goals you set for your mentoring relationship.

As the protégé, you must be adaptable – willing to reschedule appointments and accept that meetings may be interrupted. If you demonstrate inflexibility to your mentor, he may lose interest in working with you.

To demonstrate responsibility, prepare for your meetings with your mentor. Prior to the meeting, you should provide a list of questions to address.

If you fail to demonstrate responsibility by being ill-prepared, your mentor could feel that his time is being wasted. You run the risk of losing your mentor's respect and commitment to mentoring.

It's important to be persistent in asking for the amount of time you need to spend with your mentor.

Otherwise, your mentor may prioritize other tasks before your mentoring relationship.

Remember that an effective protégé is one who is responsible, dedicated, adaptable, and persistent.

Dale acted responsibly by preparing a list of questions about the cultural diversity training needs analysis and sending it to Sharon before the meeting. By doing so, he was prepared to make the most of the time he spent with her.

Had he not been prepared for the meeting, they would have not maximized their time together, and Dale may have left a bad impression on Sharon.

Dale displayed adaptability when he graciously accepted Sharon's need to interrupt their meeting.

Had he been less flexible, Sharon may have lost enthusiasm about donating her valuable time to mentoring Dale.

Enter into and maintain your mentoring relationship as an equal partner. Act in ways that prove to your mentor that you are a responsible, dedicated, adaptable, and persistent protégé.

www.ingramcontent.com/pod-product-compliance
Lightning Source LLC
Chambersburg PA
CBHW021811170526
45157CB00007B/2547